FINDING YOUR WAY
THROUGH LOSS & GRIEF

TRIGGER™
The mental health & wellbeing publisher

FINDING YOUR WAY
THROUGH LOSS & GRIEF

ABOUT THE AUTHOR

Christine Hopfgarten has been a practising psychotherapist for over a decade. She is a Cognitive Behavioural and EMDR Therapist, and Psychodynamic Psychotherapist and DIT Practitioner, specializing in trauma and relationship issues. She has worked for the London Fire Brigade's Trauma Service and a variety of NHS psychotherapy services, as well as running her own private practice.

Christine is dedicated to helping individuals find their unique way to transform their lives and reduce their psychological suffering, conflicts and problems. Her career has focused on helping many who have experienced a variety of losses to process what has happened to them and find their personal resolution and way forward.

FINDING YOUR WAY
THROUGH LOSS & GRIEF

A Therapist's Guide to Working Through Any Grieving Process

CHRISTINE HOPFGARTEN

TRIGGER™
The mental health & wellbeing publisher

This edition published in 2023 by Trigger Publishing
An imprint of Shaw Callaghan Ltd

UK Office
The Stanley Building
7 Pancras Square
Kings Cross
London N1C 4AG

US Office
On Point Executive Center, Inc
3030 N Rocky Point Drive W
Suite 150
Tampa, FL 33607
www.triggerhub.org

Text Copyright © 2021 Christine Hopfgarten
First published by Welbeck Balance in 2021

A CIP catalogue record for this book is available upon request from the British Library
ISBN: 978-1-83796-348-5
Ebook ISBN: 978-1-83796-349-2

Typeset by Lapiz Digital Services

To my three grandmothers – may your strength and
love be with me always.

And to my beloved friend Zeynep – I miss you.

CONTENTS

PROLOGUE

14 June 2017

That day, one firefighter after the other came to see me in a little room, set up only that morning when I, like everyone else in the world, heard the shocking news.

There was a strange smell in the air that felt uncomfortably overpowering; I later learnt that it was the smell of singed protective clothing. Some firefighters were completely drenched in water; all of them were completely exhausted and in shock.

Some of the stories they told me provided a glimpse of the horrific images that had burnt into their minds. But there was also numbness, confusion and a sense of comforting – yet highly alarming – detachment from reality; an odd mixture of feeling strangely calm while being at the brink of falling into the depths of human despair. Many were yearning to see their families and children; hugging and being close to them seemed to be one of the few things that would provide them with safety and comfort from the chaos that was building in their mind.

This was the day of the Grenfell Disaster.

The Grenfell Disaster was a tragic fire that resulted in the deaths of 72 people in West London. A fridge-freezer in a fourth-floor apartment of a residential tower block – Grenfell Tower – caught fire, which spread to the outside of the building, where the external cladding caused the fire to quickly spread and engulf the tower. Throughout the night, the London Fire Brigade dispatched some 40 fire engines to the scene.

The initial shock of Grenfell was only the beginning for most of the firefighters who battled the fire that night. Apart from having witnessed the most horrendous losses and deaths of others, what followed were losses of jobs, relationships, status, identity and sense of self-worth – to name only a few. What it meant to them to be a firefighter, and their confidence in being able to do what they saw as their strength and purpose, changed that day forever. While having to deal with the many losses, the trauma and overwhelming pain, they had to continue to cope while what had previously given them stability – their organization, family and structure – was also crushed by what had happened.

Working as a psychotherapist for the London Fire Brigade, I was there to support a huge number of operational staff as best I could, and I provided psychological treatment to those who needed it.

While I have been writing this book, the memory of Grenfell has faded for some, but continues to greatly affect others.

At the time of writing, a global pandemic is ongoing; it has shattered lives and caused a multitude of losses. Relationships have broken up, jobs have been lost, ill health has led to long-standing suffering and, most importantly, many lives have been tragically lost.

Grief can feel overwhelming and surreal at times. Losses continue to happen and greatly affect our lives; often it feels impossible to keep up with coming to terms with it all.

INTRODUCTION

THE PAIN AND STRUGGLES THAT ACCOMPANY LOSS

Having picked up this book, you have probably experienced a significant loss that you struggle to deal with. Your own personal loss might be due to a tragic event, or for a completely different reason. Whatever the loss, and however long ago it happened, in the midst of experiencing your loss you are likely to feel stuck, lonely, unable to cope and lost about how to begin to recover. The emotional and physical pain can be extreme, and may leave you wondering whether your reactions are normal.

Losses inflame old problems and create new ones, and often lead to people feeling overwhelmed.

If your loss happened fairly recently, you might have been asking yourself how you can cope and make sense of intensely overwhelming feelings; how you can move on from your loss, while your life feels like it has turned upside down and you are barely holding on to keep it going.

Or, you might be in disbelief about getting your life back on track if your loss has affected you for so long that you cannot even remember a time it has not been on your mind.

And how do you deal with the conflicting feelings of wanting to find happiness again, a way forward that feels alive and hopeful, while maybe not fully wanting to let go of what you have lost?

Many who are faced with major losses get stuck and are unable to cope, or struggle to fully re-engage with life, which ultimately leads to more suffering and losses. The feeling of constant failure, shame and a sense of being broken only adds to the pain.

WHAT ELSE COULD BE?

Just for a moment, I want you to allow yourself to disengage from your struggles and difficulties and visualize the following:

- You no longer feel controlled by the difficult emotions your loss is causing you, and you feel alive and hopeful again.
- You are aware of your loss and how deeply painful or upsetting it has been, but you no longer feel such emotional intensity, and your memories about your loss now belong to the past.
- Your loss no longer keeps you stuck or constrains how you feel or act in the present. You have found solutions and resolved the difficulties that previously felt insurmountable.
- You never fully have to let go of what you have lost (unless you want to), but you nevertheless feel more positive about yourself – and life – again. Even more, you have learnt valuable lessons and discovered things about yourself that make your life richer and more meaningful.

Grieving your loss will help you get here.

HOW THIS BOOK WILL BENEFIT YOU

In this book, I will guide you through a process that will help you work through your grief and reduce the distress you feel about your loss. I will start off by providing you with all the essential knowledge you need to understand your reactions and emotions, and then introduce you to several different models of grieving, which can act as a base to your own personal model. I will then help you to create the best environment in which grieving can happen, before taking you through a step-by-step structured approach to processing your loss using evidence-based interventions.

The approach I will teach you consists of:

- Defining where you want to get to
- Acceptance
- Understanding your loss
- Expressing and coping with your emotions
- Coping with and adapting to changes

Defining where you want to get to is to become clear and focused on what it is you are working toward. Holding your goals in mind helps you to access the internal and external resources that will support you to heal from your loss; it will also help you to track your progress and keep you motivated, as you will be rating how far you have come along at the end of each chapter.

Accepting all the emotions, thoughts and physical symptoms that come with grief is one of the most difficult, but important aspects to help you through your grief. Accepting does not mean giving in, but allowing yourself to move through the grieving process and learning to be with your emotions in a healthy way.

Understanding your loss entails remembering your loss and identifying what it means to you. Once you understand and acknowledge its meaning, it will be easier for you to come to terms with your loss and cope with your emotions. This also includes working on creating a balanced memory. You can only fully process and move on from something that you have made sense of and that reflects a realistic picture;

therefore your loss needs to be remembered in a coherent and balanced story.

Expressing and coping with your emotions is part of allowing yourself to feel *all* the feelings that will come up during your grieving process, without suppressing them or feeling completely overwhelmed by them. The only way you can process what has happened and start to feel better is by feeling the feelings. You will be shown how you can do so in a way that feels manageable and safe.

Coping with and adapting to changes is to take all the necessary steps to adjust to your new situation and eventually to help you to embrace your new reality.

I will also provide you with further specific insight, advice and exercises to support you with grieving specific losses.

HOW TO USE THIS BOOK

When working through this book, please do so at the pace that is just right for you – there is no need to hurry. However, remember that steady work leads to steady progress.

All exercises in this book have been proven to be useful and are evidence-based. Some might be more appealing to you than others. I would suggest you try each of them, even if you initially don't feel they will do anything for you. Sometimes the exercises that you find most challenging are the ones that will help the most. I have made the exercises as easy for you to follow as possible.

All parts of this book are relevant and you should not skip any, but you might want to take things a little slower and come back to some chapters if they feel too overwhelming at the time. Be caring and understanding toward yourself through this.

PLEASE LOOK AFTER YOURSELF

Dealing with a loss can stir up a lot of strong emotions. While feelings of deep sadness, confusion, pain and other emotions are normal and expected reactions, it's important not to force yourself to engage with any emotions and memories you do not feel comfortable with or that overwhelm you to a point that you struggle to carry on with day-to-day tasks. Listen to your inner voice about when to take things slowly and when to seek professional help.

There are certain signs and symptoms that indicate you should seek professional help, which you can find out about in more detail in chapter 9.

WHY I WROTE THIS BOOK

I am originally from Germany, but have lived in the UK for half of my life. I learnt about the powerful effects therapy can have, as well as how fascinating the mind is, very early in life. Since then, I have been on a quest to find new ways, and to refine those ways I already have, of understanding and helping individuals with their psychological suffering, conflicts and problems. I deeply care about how I affect those I work with, and continue to be fascinated by the transformation individuals can go through on a psychological level. I feel humbled and honoured to be part of what enables people to turn their lives around – even if I am only a very tiny part that makes all the difference.

As a psychotherapist working for the London Fire Brigade and the UK National Health Service and in private practice, I have heard the unique stories of many who have experienced a variety of losses. I have helped many to process what has happened to them and find their personal resolution and way forward.

My early postgraduate studies included psychodynamic psychotherapy and cognitive behavioural therapy, and I have since specialized in a more relational approach, including training in dynamic interpersonal therapy and trauma-focused therapy, especially Eye Movement Desensitization and Reprocessing (EMDR).

As a therapist, I believe that it is important to deeply engage on a relational and emotional level – to help people understand the connections and causes of their difficulties – while also using ample practical and structured interventions and exercises to help individuals deal with their problems. I trust that the best approach to help you grieve your loss and to help you achieve happiness and contentment is to draw on evidence-based therapies and psychological models, while also focusing on, and attuning to, what makes you unique and different. I believe that to get better, you need to address the past, as well as the present.

MOVING FORWARD

Please be aware that the approach to grieving your loss in this book is not a quick fix. It is likely that your progress will be steady, but may sometimes decline before improving again. It will take time for you to see full progress, but you should start to feel some improvement from the beginning.

What you can expect from this book is a thorough and extensive guide that will help you understand, cope and work through your loss. It will help you to structure your life and give you all the tools you need to grieve your loss and feel good about yourself, and life, again.

The techniques and insights I will teach you will not only help with your grieving, but they will be invaluable skills that will enable you to deal with a range of other emotional problems and difficulties.

PART 1

WORKING THROUGH
LOSS AND GRIEF

1

UNDERSTANDING LOSS
AND GRIEF

There will be a particular loss, or perhaps even more than one, that has brought you to this book. One that has probably touched you deeply and you are finding difficult to come to terms with.

Whatever loss you have experienced, this book can help you to make sense of it, to understand yourself better, to understand why this loss means so much to you, to find a way through those difficult and overwhelming feelings, and to help you on the path to creating a more content life for yourself.

There are many types of losses, and I want to explain what we mean by "loss" and "grief", why we need to grieve, and what purpose these overwhelming, confusing and uncomfortable feelings have in the first place. We will then look at the grieving process, to help you understand what your experience of grieving might be and what you can realistically expect from yourself. Finally, we will look at the positive changes that can come from working through your grief.

WHAT IS LOSS AND GRIEF?

Loss is defined as the process of losing someone or something. It is normal to have an intense emotional reaction to losing someone who you were close to or losing something that was of value to you. In this book we use the word "loss" to refer to *the process of your loss*, including what led up to your loss, the actual experience of your loss, as well as dealing with the consequences of your loss.

Grief is the response to the loss of someone you were attached to or something that was of great value to you. When we talk about grief in this book, we refer to emotional, behavioural, physical and cognitive reactions to loss. Grieving can be thought of as a process that helps you to come to terms with your loss on a physical and emotional level. Grief and the grieving process are necessary to process loss and to feel better about yourself and your life again.

EVOLUTION AND WHY WE NEED TO GRIEVE

When we lose someone or something important in our life, it is painful and difficult because whoever or whatever we have lost was part of our identity. We are defined by our relationships, our roles and the places and social circles we feel we belong to. Our wellbeing relies on close bonds with other people. It is therefore no surprise that a loss – a threat to our identity – can consume us and create anxiety, anger, confusion and depression.

Attachment theory tells us that humans depend and thrive on deep and enduring emotional bonds with other humans. When a baby is born, they are completely helpless and their life depends on a caregiver for food, warmth and protection, but also for emotional and social development. When babies experience separation from, or the loss of, the mother or those they have affectionate bonds with, they experience and show intense distress until they are reunited. If the absence becomes prolonged, the baby eventually gives up and turns quiet – from an evolutionary perspective, if "Mummy" is gone, it is safer to hide away to keep safe. Without close and secure attachments, the world is a dangerous place. Our brains have developed to thrive, and we need social connections as a survival strategy. Our social nature and need for attachment drive us to make close bonds and connections. Belonging, and being attached to others, equals protection.

When we lose one of our close connections, it is therefore not surprising it is painful. Every cell in our body tries to maintain close relationships for survival and avoid loss at any cost. Evolutionarily, it makes sense that loss is so difficult and painful – if it was easy, it would make us very vulnerable.

When we grow up, our attachments spread to siblings, friends, colleagues at work, those who share the same interests. Our protective circle widens and hence provides us with more security.

Growing up, we also learn who we are through the relationships we have. Our identity is – to a great extent – a reflection and assimilation of all those relationships. We are greatly invested in our identity as it gives us a sense of knowing where we stand and what we can expect from others and from ourselves in life – it organizes our internal world.[1] Our identity is reflected in the jobs we choose and what type of life we live. Hence, when we experience a loss in areas closely linked to our identity, such as our job, we experience similar feelings to those of losing a relationship. These feelings are a result of the actual relationships you lose, together with the loss of parts of yourself – for example, when you lose your job, you lose the relationships you have with your colleagues and your clients, and you can also lose a sense of security, financial freedom, respect, and purpose.

Loss will cause most to feel an urge to withdraw from life, and to experience feelings similar to depression, at least during the most acute phase. Depression – from an evolutionary point – is a threat protection response.[2] When our safety and identity is at threat, our brains force us to stay safe "by hiding away until things seem safer again". Depression is a form of a "shut down", as a result of a change in the amygdala, the part of our brain responsible for the perception of feelings, which makes us more sensitive to detecting and responding to threats. So, feeling depressed for some time after experiencing a loss is completely understandable. Taking some time for yourself, or only being in contact with those who are closest to you, is often needed to make sense of what has happened to you and to get your confidence back.

TYPES OF LOSS

When we hear about loss and grief, we often tend to think about bereavement. However, we experience so many other losses in life; you might be surprised to find out how many losses you have experienced and worked through already in your life.

Losses are often about **losing a person** who was important and close to you. Losing your mother, father, partner or child through **death** can be the most painful experience you can go through. But you might also lose a loved one through the **break-up of a relationship**, **estrangement**, or **illness**. Loss does not necessarily mean someone is no longer alive, but they may nevertheless no longer be part of your life, or at least not as they used to be. Many people are surprised by the intensity of their feelings when they experience the loss of a person or relationship when the other person is still alive. They are confused, as they feel it should not feel like they have actually died. The truth is that, internally, it *can* feel just like that.

Losing your job can happen in many different ways. While it is usually easier to lose your job when you are the one deciding to quit, it might nevertheless be difficult if you feel you have little choice, for example due to your age or other circumstances out of your control. As mentioned, losing your job can be a very defining loss as you lose all the aspects you felt the job provided you with, such as income, identity, a sense of belonging and purpose.

Illness and loss of health can be a huge loss, as you have to grieve the future you had imagined with your healthy self. It will be even more difficult to come to terms with if the condition is incurable and possibly fatal. What is lost, even if only temporarily, might be so many aspects of yourself – such as your confidence, your independence, your power and your purpose.

If you are experiencing **fertility problems** or have had a **miscarriage**, you might struggle with the loss of your ability to create a child with your partner, and what this might mean to you as a woman or a man. Regardless of how old your baby was when the miscarriage happened, the loss can often feel as horrendous as if the loss had occurred after they had been born.

SECONDARY LOSSES

Losing a person or a part of yourself and your identity that was of value to you always leads to other losses in your life, which will need to be grieved and addressed. Your primary loss might have led you to lose any of these aspects that are connected to your relationships and identity:

**income confidence memory
security trust purpose in life sex-life
culture sense of belonging respect power
purpose innocence independence role
self-worth acceptance value safety
... and many others**

Some of the losses you experience in life might feel less tangible, but are nevertheless important and can impact you just as much as more obvious losses. These will be **losses of hopes and fantasies**. This may be a romantic relationship that never developed or the exciting career you never managed to have. You might have had hopes and dreams growing up that were shattered. Perhaps you have also come to realize that your view of someone, maybe your parents, might have been idealized and not who they really are. Regardless of whether there is an actual loss or a loss happening in your mind, you still need to grieve what you imagined was going to happen or what was your truth. It might be difficult to accept and admit that losses of hopes and fantasies can affect you so deeply, but we are built to grieve these just as we do actual losses, as they hold so much meaning and importance for us.

We will take a closer look at certain common losses in Part 2, but *any loss that has brought you to read this book is valid*, and all the advice and tools given in this book will be useful and relevant in your grieving process.

THE GRIEVING PROCESS

Let's look at what your expectations and beliefs about loss and grief are before we go into more detail about what you might experience during your grieving process.

In general, a lot of people in our society, surrounded by current cultural influences, will expect that the grieving process should be a lot shorter than it actually is. You might feel that "You shouldn't *still* be crying" or "You should be better by now", and you might come under pressure from others to get over your loss and start acting like your old self again.

You might have expectations about how your grieving should look and whether you should be grieving on your own or sharing your grief with others. You might expect that you need to spend a lot of time thinking about what you have lost. Or, you might try not to think about it as you worry it will just make things worse, so you keep yourself busy. You might expect certain feelings, such as sadness or numbness, but will be surprised about other feelings, such as intense anger or relief.

THERE IS NO WRONG WAY TO GRIEVE

When it comes to grieving, everyone's different – and you cannot grieve incorrectly. You will get to know your own particular way of grieving by using this book. Your personality style and ways of coping with life will guide you to identify how best to move forward and feel good about yourself and life again.

Certain coping strategies, particularly avoidance (which we will address in later chapters), will make the grieving process longer and more difficult to get through. However, there are other coping strategies, which I will teach you, that make the grieving process easier and quicker. I want to help you find your unique grieving style that will help you to get to a place where you feel more content and at peace with yourself and your loss.

EMOTIONAL AND PHYSICAL RESPONSES TO LOSS

When you have experienced a loss, you will experience a range of emotions that may come and go or change from one into another. You can expect to feel unmotivated, less tolerant of others, wanting to withdraw from others or not wanting to be alone. You might feel tired, have difficulty concentrating, cry easily and not be in control of your emotions. All of this might make you feel there is something wrong with you and that you will not able to get through this. All of those feelings are normal; they will pass and you will feel better again.

Grief can be confusing and often does not happen in a linear fashion. Lots of people feel that grief happens in waves, with intense phases and calmer phases that follow each other. This can feel unsettling and disappointing as you might think you are "better" and then be hit by another strong upsetting feeling, which makes you feel as if you are going backwards. Rest assured that this is normal and you are not getting worse.

When grieving, some people will need to keep active, while others need to slow down and withdraw from life for some time. Some of us experience delayed grief, as we are unable to face it at the time. All of this is okay, as long as you recognize and accept that there will come a time that you will need to face the feelings and experiences that come with your grief.

The Early Stages

In general, your emotional and physical reactions to your loss are usually strongest soon after your loss, and they will slowly reduce in intensity over time. After the initial shock wears off and the reality of the loss sinks in, grief can hit very hard; you may lose interest in life and be unable to relax, and have sleep problems. In this early stage, many people feel the need to turn completely inward. If you feel like this, or have felt like this, make sure you give yourself this time; don't let others pressure you to reconnect with the world immediately. In some days or weeks, you will return to sleeping and eating more regularly, and you will start to enjoy some of the things you used to again.

Different feelings will emerge and change through your grieving process, such as feeling numb, low, sad, anxious, depressed, confused and angry. Often people experience intense emotional and, sometimes, physical pain, especially in the early stages. Sadness and emotional pain are often experienced as the strongest and most long-lasting feelings; but, depending on your loss, you might also have anger as your primary feeling, or you might be confused or numb.

Common Physical and Emotional Reactions

You can probably relate to how unsurmountable the task of grieving can feel, and it is indeed a huge task for our mind and body. Apart from being aware of your emotions, you might also notice physical reactions, either in addition to or as a result of your emotional reactions.

The box below lists the common physical and emotional reactions to loss. Spend some time thinking about which reactions you have noticed in yourself, which you find easy and which you find most difficult. You might want to revisit this list while you are working through your grief, to help you identify what you are feeling and to help you see how no feelings last forever.

EMOTIONAL AND PHYSICAL REACTIONS

Emotional Reactions

Sadness, anxiety, panic, guilt, anger, lack of motivation, hopelessness, shock, disbelief, regret, peace, emptiness, pining/yearning, confusion, relief, shame, denial, resistance.

Physical Reactions

Muscle tension, heart racing, headaches, aches and pains, difficulty sleeping, loss of or increased appetite, sleeping more than usual, agitation, restlessness, gastrointestinal disturbances such as stomach cramps or nausea, fatigue, difficulty concentrating, dizziness, feeling detached from surroundings and people.

Sometimes the feelings you experience might conflict or feel overwhelming. These moments and phases are very difficult to go through, and the grieving process can leave you feeling as though you have little control over what is happening. Remember that, although tough, it is completely normal to have these experiences and these moments will not last forever. I will help you face your emotions and get you through these difficult phases in the following chapters.

You might be surprised to see feelings such as "relief" and "peace" in the list of emotional reactions to grief. Feeling a sense of relief can sometimes provoke shame or guilt, but having these feelings does not mean that you are a bad person or that you do not honour what has been lost; they are common and valid feelings that come after something that was tremendously difficult has ended.

You might also experience a denial of the loss or a reluctance to grieve, which is often fuelled by the dilemma loss poses: on one hand we want to move forward in life and leave our loss behind, on the other hand we don't want to let go of the life we had before.

Remember, your grieving is unlikely to be linear; there will be ups and downs and progress will sometimes be slow. Don't be discouraged – you are doing everything right and you will feel better for longer periods very soon.

THE TIME IT TAKES TO GRIEVE

How long might someone expect to grieve? This question does not have a clear and defined answer; there is no time frame to work toward. How long you will grieve depends on several factors, including:

- What the person or what you have lost meant to you.
- What else is going on in your life at the moment, and how much time you have to let yourself grieve, or whether your grief is/was "delayed".
- How much support you have, and if you are generally feeling settled in other areas of your life.

Grieving can last a few months or several years. Some people find that their grief never fully ends, but they reach a place where they feel content with their grief always being part of their life. Don't focus too much on time, as it might feel overwhelming for you right now to look into the future. You might put yourself under pressure or be disappointed with yourself if you are not feeling a certain way by a certain time. Focus on taking it day by day, then week by week, and soon you will see things starting to get easier again.

This book will help you to realize that grieving is very hard and draining at times, but that there will be times during the grieving process when you may actually feel okay and able to find energy and focus.

COPING WITH AND ADAPTING TO CHANGE

An important later stage of the grieving process is to deal with and adapt to the changes that were the consequences of your loss (see chapter 8). Every loss brings change, and getting used to your new situation and roles requires time for new learning and adjustment. Keep in mind that change is difficult for most of us, but particularly so when we are experiencing strong and sometimes debilitating feelings in relation to loss. Struggling with change is absolutely normal, so have realistic expectations of yourself about how long it will take to adapt to your changes, and about the amount of support you will need.

THE BENEFITS OF GRIEVING YOUR LOSS

Grieving can be thought of as a process that helps you to come to terms with your loss on a physical and emotional level. Grieving gives you the time and space to process all the emotions and memories related to your loss and to learn to live without what has been lost. It will also help you to reconcile how your life is now different from the way you expected it to be.

Whatever your loss, it will be with you and will affect you always. What will change is how you feel about it – and about yourself – in relation to your loss. You will get to a place where the changes that were initially so overwhelming and impossible to accept will feel okay and normal, and you might even be able to look back and appreciate how you have grown as a result of the loss.

Your reward for going through the grieving process can be an inner healing through learning ways of coping with your emotions that allow you to access joyful feelings again, feelings that will have been suppressed or which temporarily disappeared in the shadows of your grief.

It *is* possible to learn to live without what you have lost. This may be difficult to believe if you are at the beginning or stuck in your grieving process, but you *will* find meaning again and get back to your normal or "new normal" self.

Many psychological studies have shown that when people are able to work through a traumatic experience – and any loss that affects you deeply on an emotional and physical level is traumatic – they experience "post-traumatic growth".[3] This growth leads to further insights, internal changes and a new-found sense of wellbeing and energy, which go beyond how someone felt before the trauma happened. You, too, are able to experience this. Just be patient and trust yourself, and you will get there.

PERCEPTIONS OF LOSS AND GRIEF IN OUR SOCIETY

Many people find it difficult to talk about their loss, and feel that they do not want to bring others down by telling them about their painful feelings and thoughts. It can sometimes be a challenge to find someone who you feel truly understands and acknowledges what you are going through. Some of this might be due to your perception, as you might feel very vulnerable and fear others rejecting you and what you have to say. This is completely understandable and, as we have seen when we talked about evolution, it's just the way your brain works in order to protect you.

However, apart from how your experience might be coloured by your feelings at the moment, it is also true that our society can find it difficult to support those who are grieving. Our society, advertising and social media is so focused on success and gains, it can easily feel wrong that we should feel any pain, particularly for a long time.

You might find that talking to others about what you are going through touches on feelings they find difficult to be with or express. People will often try to fix things or tell you something positive to cheer you up; but when you are grieving this can feel like they do not understand or do not want to hear what you are going through. You might hear things such as, "There is a reason for everything", "Life is not fair" or "You are better off without him/her anyway". People usually mean well, but it can make you feel deeply misunderstood. Unfortunately, the need for others in our society to make things better and to change this painful feeling into something "lighter" as quickly as possible can be pervasive.

The difficulty our society has with painful feelings, loss and grieving is something you cannot change. But by being aware that this is the case will help you to not take things too personally when you are given unhelpful advice or feel that someone is not wanting to listen to you. It will also help you to look for those who *will* understand. Do tell people what you need – many will appreciate your instructions, as it will make them feel less anxious about saying the wrong thing or not being helpful enough.

CHAPTER SUMMARY

- Our identity and safety as human beings is closely linked to the people and aspects of our life we are attached to, and any loss of the latter will pose a threat to our identity and sense of safety.
- Grieving is an evolutionary, adaptive response to loss.
- There are many types of losses in life that we will need to grieve.
- It's normal to have an intense and sometimes overwhelming emotional response to experiencing a loss, particularly in the early stages of grief.
- There are many emotional reactions to loss, and some of these might be overwhelming, conflicting or confusing.
- All emotional reactions, including relief, are valid and common – none are wrong.
- Physical reactions to loss, such as sleep problems, tension, aches and pains and tiredness, are very common.
- Denial of the loss, or resistance to grieving, is understandable considering what a difficult and exhausting task grieving is.
- Grieving happens in waves and not in a linear fashion.
- Adapting to the changes that are the consequences of your loss is an essential stage in your grieving process.
- Grieving helps you to come to terms with your loss on an emotional and physical level.
- It is possible to grieve any loss and to find meaning and happiness in life again.
- Many people who have worked through a difficult grieving experience find that they have grown as a person and have made positive internal and external changes – this is post-traumatic growth.

2

MODELS OF GRIEVING

Grief can be deeply unsettling and destabilizing. You probably often wish that things would just be normal again, and feel at your most vulnerable; or you might be feeling very numb or angry. As mentioned in chapter 1, there are many different emotions you might experience when grieving.

Researchers and professionals who work in the field of bereavement (but any loss, regardless of how it occurs, will have a similar impact on you) and helping people with their losses have looked into the process of grieving to help make sense of what people go through after a loss.

HOW MODELS OF GRIEVING CAN HELP YOU

Giving what you are going through, a framework can help you to feel less overwhelmed, and knowing a particular feeling is not going to last forever can make it easier to stay with that feeling or experience. Recognizing different phases can also provide you with some comfort that what you are experiencing is normal. However, while these models can help you understand and make sense of what you are going through, they are by no means instructive or prescriptive of every grieving process. Your grieving process is unique; there is no particular order to these phases, nor does everyone go through every phase (at

19

least not with the same intensity). It's best to understand the following models as a map – something to give you direction and orientation. There are many different paths to get to the same destination, and sometimes you might have to go back and forth a few times or struggle up a hill before you can finally move onward.

THE DIFFERENT MODELS OF GRIEVING

I will briefly mention Elisabeth Kübler-Ross's well-known model of grief and then present three other models of grieving; each focuses on slightly different aspects of the grieving process, while also sharing many similarities. You might be drawn more to one model if it resonates with how you understand and generally think about yourself and life.

THE FIVE STAGES OF GRIEF

Elisabeth Kübler-Ross first presented her renowned stage model of grief in her 1969 book, *On Death and Dying*.[4] The five stages of Kübler-Ross's loss model are:

1. **Denial**
2. **Anger**
3. **Bargaining**
4. **Depression**
5. **Acceptance**

While this model takes account of the themes many experience during their grieving process, it is now widely acknowledged that grieving does not happen in fixed stages. Furthermore, Kübler-Ross's model does not address the full physical, psychological and social aspects of grieving, and lacks emphasis on the restorative aspects of grieving.

THE SIX 'R'S OF MOURNING

The Six 'R's of Mourning is a theory of the grieving process developed by Therese Rando.[5] The model is made up of six separate tasks, grouped into three phases – avoidance, confrontation and accommodation – which form the mourning process.

1. During **avoidance**, you might not want or feel ready to face the reality of the loss, or to think about it. The task during this phase is to "**Recognize the loss**". This means you need to come to understand what has happened to you and really accept it.
2. The **confrontation** phase involves dealing with your grief and finding ways to process what you are experiencing. The first task in this phase is to "**React to the separation**". This means to fully embrace and accept all the different feelings one experiences while grieving, as well as acknowledging secondary losses, such as financial security, confidence and purpose. The second task is to "**Recollect and re-experience**", which involves remembering all the good and all the difficult memories about the relationship or the experiences you had, and building a balanced memory. This will become part of how you will remember what you have lost and how it will influence you going forward. The third task in this phase is to "**Relinquish old attachments**". This does not mean that one needs to fully move on and forget old attachments, but is about getting used to and accepting the absence of what has been lost.
3. The final phase – **accommodation** – is all about finding meaning in life again. The first task in this phase is to "**Readjust to the new world without forgetting the old world**". It involves readjusting to your new roles and circumstances, and appreciating how you might have changed as a person as a result of your loss. While you are

getting used to your new life, you are still remembering what you have lost in a valuable way. The second task in this phase is to **"Reinvest emotional energy"**.

This is about investing emotional energy in current relationships and projects, or perhaps even new ones, and rediscovering a sense of purpose. It is not about replacing what has been lost, but allowing yourself to make space for new things and to enjoy them.

THE DUAL PROCESS MODEL OF GRIEVING

The Dual Process Model of Grief by Margaret Stroebe and Henk Schut describes grief as a "dynamic, regulatory coping process of oscillation between two contrasting modes of functioning: loss orientation mode and restoration orientation mode".[6] In loss orientation mode, the griever engages in thoughts, emotions, actions and memories related to their loss, while often turning away from their current life. In the restoration orientation mode, the griever engages with actions, thoughts and emotions related to their current and new life, including adapting to their changes and engaging with new roles, while also at times distracting themselves from their grief or avoiding emotions related to their loss.

Stroebe and Schut's model stresses that temporary avoidance and denial of grief is part of a normal and healthy grieving response, and can be adaptive and restoration-focused. Their model also highlights that grieving does not occupy all of a person's time, but that these two coping modes are embedded in the activities and experiences of everyday life, such as talking with friends and family about other topics than the loss, watching TV or doing household chores.

EVERYDAY LIFE EXPERIENCES AND ACTIVITIES	
LOSS-ORIENTED	**RESTORATION-ORIENTED**
Remembering and processing happy and painful memories about the loss	Adjusting to changes
Turning away from current life and life changes	Denial/avoidance of grief
Engaging in thoughts, actions and emotions related to the loss	Developing new roles/identities and relationships

Table Showing the Dual Process Model of Grief, adapted from Stroebe & Schut, "The dual process model of coping with bereavement: rationale and description"[7]

WORDEN'S TASKS OF GRIEVING

J W Worden's succinct model of grief sees grieving as an active process involving engagement with four tasks:[8]

1. **Accept** the reality of the loss.
2. **Process** the pain of grief.
3. **Adjust** to a world without the deceased.
    a) External adjustments – daily living
    b) Internal adjustments – who am I now?
    c) Spiritual adjustments – finding meaning, new assumptive world
4. **Find** enduring connection with the deceased while embarking on a new life. (This last aspect might differ for other types of loss, and may not be relevant to all losses.)

Worden points out that these four tasks do not have to be completed in order, and might be dealt with separately or alongside each other. He also stresses that an individual's response to loss is influenced by external and internal factors, such as the person's previous relationship to who or what has been lost, other current life stressors, or how the loss happened. These factors need to be taken into account to fully understand and appreciate a person's individual response to their loss and how they might approach their grieving process.

Please note, these models should *not* be taken as a literal description of what you are or will experience, but can give you a good idea of what to expect from your grieving process and where you might get to. Do not worry about spending "too little" or "too much" time working on one task, and you do not have to wait for the phases to occur, or make them happen – trust that, as long as you are open toward your feelings, listen to yourself and take an active approach to grieving, each phase and process will happen naturally. Working through this book will help you to move through your grief and you will feel more comfortable with the process, so it becomes something you feel confident in.

Bear in mind that completing all tasks or phases is not the ultimate goal of grieving and would be unrealistic. Some people continue to struggle to fully adjust to their new world, even when they feel they have reached the end of their main grieving process, and are instead content with where they got to. Others fully adjust to their new reality and are no longer affected by their loss after they have grieved for it. The reality is that grieving is a complex process that isn't as neat as we might wish it to be, and does not lead us to a well-defined ending or goal. What *is* important is that you identify what it is you would like (and are ready) to change, and that you define your grieving process as whatever you want it to be. The aim is to feel more at peace with your loss and good about yourself and your life again. How many tasks of grieving you need to complete to get there is something you will find out yourself and is not defined by models, only by you.

The following case study illustrates Evelina's grieving process and the feelings and physical symptoms she experienced during this time. Evelina's story of losing both her partner and her job will give you a good idea of how the above models of grieving can look in real life, as well as the emotions and reactions that can be experienced.

EVELINA'S STORY

Evelina was 42 when she lost her partner, Max. He had been having problems with drinking for a while and eventually died from complications and organ failure. It was quite a shock to Evelina as, although she had been aware of the problem and had tried to make him seek help, Max was good at covering up his problems, especially at work and in front of his friends. As such, she never realized quite how seriously his health had been affected by his drinking.

Shortly after her bereavement, Evelina left her job at an advertising company. She had not enjoyed her role or the dynamics in her team for a while, and the loss of her partner finally made her feel unable to face the problems at work. She handed in her notice during her bereavement leave. While she initially felt a huge sense of relief, the loss of financial security and routine left her anxious about her decision.

She spent a lot of time at home thinking about what had happened, and was tormented by the feeling she had not done enough to save her partner and get him help. The guilt and sadness became unbearable, and she tried to keep herself busy so there was less time to think and feel bad about her situation. She struggled to sleep or focus on anything, and nothing gave her pleasure. She felt tired all day long, but found it impossible to rest and relax. When she would eventually fall asleep, she would sometimes wake up from nightmares.

After four months had passed, she found herself asking herself, "Why can't I get over this? It's been too long! I cannot see a way to ever get over this!" She found crying about her loss very draining, and feared her sadness would never end if she were to let it surface fully. However, after some time she realized that when she did cry, in time she always stopped; also, when she let herself cry, eventually the times she felt like crying became less and less.

Her feelings changed from guilt to anger toward both her partner and her work, and toward the unfairness of life. As more time passed, Evelina realized that there was no running away or avoiding the reality of her losses and how her life had changed forever. She decided to fight the tears and feelings less, and made time to engage with her emotions. She started to talk more about how she felt and decided that it did not really matter how much she cried or looked vulnerable in front of others.

From then on, although things were still very up and down and Evelina had periods where she tried to cope with her feelings by drinking too much and watching Netflix for days on end, she always managed to get back to realizing that making sense of what the loss meant to her and dealing with her emotions was the only way forward. With time, this allowed her to feel lighter again, and difficult thoughts and feelings about her partner became less and less frequent. She no longer thought about her former job; she even joined a smaller advertising company and started to feel creative and valued at work again.

After two years, there are still things Evelina finds very difficult about her relationship with Max and the circumstances of his death, but she also has a lot of good memories she now cherishes. She has come to the realization that there was probably not a lot she could have done to save Max. She *feels more comfortable admitting that, while she very much misses Max's lively and loving character, she also feels a sense of relief about no longer having to go through the fights, sadness and drama around his drinking.*

Evelina is not quite ready for a new relationship, but she now feels much clearer about what she wants and needs from a partner. Reflecting and engaging with herself about her loss has made her more determined to seek out healthier relationships in the future.

CHAPTER SUMMARY

- Models of grieving can give you direction and orientation throughout your grieving process, and help you feel less overwhelmed and lost.
- There are different models of grieving, and you will likely be drawn more to one of the models than the others as it will resonate with how you understand and generally think about yourself and life.
- Grieving is a dynamic and complex process, and there is no particular order in which to grieve.
- Completing all tasks or phases as outlined by the different models is not the ultimate goal of grieving and would be unrealistic.
- What will need to be part of your grieving process is not defined by any models, but by yourself.

3

PREPARATION IS KEY

Preparing and setting yourself up for your grief work is extremely important, and should not be underestimated. The steps suggested in this chapter will allow you to build a strong internal and external support system to help you work through your difficult emotions and tolerate difficulties should they arise, rather than becoming overwhelmed by them.

To help you get set up, we will cover four areas:

- Self-care
- Scheduled grieving time
- Writing things down
- A social support system

Please spend some time on each area, and make sure you are satisfied with where you are at in each of them. Make or plan changes as needed. We are not looking for perfection, and "good enough" is always the best goal to strive for. I understand that you might not want to spend too much time on this foundation work, but bear in mind that preparation is often key – it will make working through the rest of this book much easier.

YOUR SELF-CARE PLAN

Looking after yourself and your basic needs is really very important, especially when you are going through a difficult time emotionally. Sometimes, you might just feel too tired and exhausted to do what is best for your body and mind, or you might feel like you do not deserve to be looked after if your self-esteem has been badly affected by your loss. It can also be painful to carry on with life and your usual self-care routines, as they can be a powerful reminder of how life was before your loss.

As hard it may be, do your best to look after yourself. It does not have to be as well as you look after yourself usually if this is still too difficult, but if you change at least a few things that are lacking and aim for the best you can, it will be a huge step toward getting better.

It is easy to forget what good self-care looks like, so here are some basics that will help you come up with your own self-care plan going forward.

Nutrition
Eat healthy and balanced meals. It's completely normal to eat more or less on some days, but watch out for not eating enough, or comfort eating for long periods of time. Drink enough water to stay hydrated, and keep your energy levels up.

Sleep
Get enough sleep, ideally seven to nine hours each night, and avoid oversleeping. Don't go to sleep too late; ideally, head to bed before 11pm.

Exercise
Do at least 20 to 30 minutes of exercise a day. Choose an exercise you enjoy and that makes you feel good. Walking is

exercise, so it is easy to incorporate into your day; for example, you might walk to work instead of taking the train or car.

Pleasurable activities

Make a list of six things you loved, or still love, to do. Don't worry if you feel they will no longer give you as much pleasure as they used to right now. Do at least one of them each week, even if you are not feeling as excited and motivated about them right now; experiencing even a little pleasure is better than no pleasure at all. With time, your levels of enjoyment and motivation will return, and they will return more easily if you keep doing these activities.

Alcohol and drugs

Go easy on alcohol and other drugs. Alcohol increases depression and makes it much harder to deal with your problems in the long term. Stay away from drugs, as they mess with all sorts of feelings and physiological processes, and will make you more emotionally imbalanced and overwhelmed in the long run.

Balance

Remember the importance of keeping balance in your life. Balance is imperative in everything we do, and it is usually not useful to do things to the extreme. It will not help you to constantly be doing things that feel easy and relaxing, such as watching Netflix or browsing social media, and hardly spending any time on being with your difficult feelings related to your grief. Likewise, spending all day, every day, thinking, reflecting and talking about your pain and your loss is probably not going to be helpful either. It is usually also unhelpful to go from no social contact to suddenly attending every social gathering or party in the midst of working through a loss. .

Remember to keep a balance between home, work and leisure; between time with others and time by yourself; and between "active grieving time" and time spent doing pleasurable or ordinary things that have nothing to do with your loss.

Routine

It's good to stick to a basic routine. Sometimes, you might need to take some time away from everything, and that is absolutely okay. However, generally sticking to a routine will help you to feel safe and grounded. Sometimes, having things to do can get you through a difficult day. A routine also keeps you in touch with day-to-day life, your feelings and those around you – preventing you from becoming isolated in the long term. Most importantly, routine helps as it eliminates the decision-making process, which can be especially onerous if you are already struggling with motivation and feeling lost. Being able to do things automatically helps to conserve your limited energy. Taking small steps is the key – little things, such as making your bed each day and preparing regular meals for yourself – are an important part of your routine.

Emotional Self-care

Good self-care also includes how you treat yourself on an emotional level. I advise you to be as kind and patient as you can toward yourself throughout the time you are grieving. This is a very difficult time for you, and you deserve all the time and kindness you can possibly give yourself right now. Neglecting yourself or being critical and impatient is never a good strategy, and even more so right now. Don't worry if you are still finding this difficult – many people struggle with looking after themselves well on an emotional level. As long as you have an intention to work toward good emotional self-care, you are on the right path.

EXERCISE
Setting Up a Positive and Realistic Self-care Routine

1. Take a minute to reflect on what your current self-care looks like and the areas you feel you need to work on, referring to the list of basics I've just outlined.
2. Come up with a self-care routine and make a note of it. It does not need to be long or complicated, but should include the things you know are good for you and are relatively easy to stick to.
3. If you don't feel confident about being able to stick to the plan, then simplify it; you can add to it at a later stage when you feel emotionally and physically ready.
4. If you are feeling very low and have been doing very little recently, it will help you to tick off each part of your routine every day to start with; this will help you get back on track and feel a sense of accomplishment.
5. In the first few weeks, leave yourself reminders of your new self-care routine until it becomes habit.

GRIEVING TIME

It is important that you schedule some time on a regular basis to allow for your grieving. Set-aside time will give you a greater sense of control over processing your loss, and gives space to the feelings that will arise; this will help you to avoid being overcome by your grief suddenly when you are unprepared. It doesn't mean you will never have strong feelings about your loss outside this time. However, with a dedicated grieving time allocated, it is often easier to contain your grief and carry on until your allocated time. By dedicating time solely to your grieving, it also sends a clear message to your brain that grieving is important and that you are looking after yourself and your feelings.

It's easiest to schedule in grieving time for 20 to 40 minutes every day to start off with. This might sound like a lot, but dedicating time to yourself and working through your loss will be far more beneficial to you than watching TV, or browsing the internet or social media. Consider when in the day is the best time for you to work on processing your loss. Over time, your grieving time will reduce; you will notice this as you start to feel better in yourself and naturally think less often about your loss.

WHAT YOU CAN DO DURING YOUR GRIEVING TIME

- Read this book.
- Reflect on what you have read, and write down your answers to the exercises in this book.
- Write in your journal (we'll cover this in a moment).
- Meditation and mindfulness practices around your loss.
- Revisit situations and experiences from your day that brought on memories or strong feelings about your loss.
- Talk to others about your loss.
- Do activities that help you find closure.
- Spend time acknowledging and being with your feelings.
- Spend time trying to understand and make sense of memories and feelings.
- Use a creative outlet, such as painting, poetry or music.
- Play music or watch a movie that reminds you of the person you have lost.
- Talk to the person you have lost, as though they are sitting next to you.

• Go for a walk or find a beautiful spot in nature that helps you feel at peace and connected to who you have lost or what you have lost in a positive way, without getting overwhelmed.

There are plenty of things you can do to help you with your grieving; choosing three or four activities will help you get started until you find out naturally what comforts and supports you the most.

WRITING THINGS DOWN

Now that you have your routine set up and your grieving time scheduled in, let's look at how you can make the best use of this book by writing things down.

Writing things down to help you identify and manage your feelings and thought processes is really very useful. When you feel stuck or overwhelmed by your feelings and what is going on in your mind, writing down what is going on for you or what you need can help you gain some control in a difficult situation; it can help you gain insight into what you are experiencing and find resolutions to your problems.

People can feel quite differently about writing things down. You might have experience of writing a journal, or you might be someone who feels uncomfortable about having your personal thoughts and feelings written down somewhere. I would like you to try and keep an open mind and just give it a go. There are lots of benefits to writing things down (particularly your responses to the exercises in this book), whereas only thinking things through in your head will make it harder for you to make progress with your grief.

WHY WRITING THINGS DOWN IS HELPFUL

- It helps you to slow down your thoughts and really focus on what is going on in your mind, without feeling overwhelmed and confused. It can help you to stop going round in circles with your thoughts.
- It helps you to stay focused on identifying what you are feeling and thinking; you are much less likely to become distracted and lose focus when writing things down.
- Making a conscious effort to write down your thoughts and feelings helps you to view things and think in a different way. Sometimes, it will help you to understand yourself better and to gain clarity about what you are experiencing and how to move forward.
- Writing things down helps you to distance yourself from your thoughts and emotions as you have to focus on the process of writing. Distancing will make the thoughts less powerful and overwhelming and you will feel more able to cope with them.
- Writing down how you feel or have felt helps in accepting and acknowledging what is upsetting you. As you will see in the following chapter, acceptance and acknowledgement are crucial in helping you manage your emotions.

HOW TO WRITE THINGS DOWN

You can write things down wherever you wish – in a dedicated journal, on your computer or phone, or on pieces of paper that you collect in a folder. Choose whichever medium makes you feel most comfortable and is accessible. Lots of people find journals the most useful medium, as it is easy to flick through previous pages and revisit what you have written – and there is something very personal and emotive about writing things by hand. However, if you feel more comfortable writing things on your computer or phone, then go with that. Do whatever feels right, but please write things down. I guarantee it will benefit you, and you will be surprised by your progress when you look through your notes after some time. Remember to date your entries, as it will help you see your progress, and help your mind organize your grieving experiences in a timeline and give it some structure.

As suggested, set aside some dedicated grieving time, at least until you notice some consistent improvement in yourself, and use this time to write things down. At the beginning, it's best to write regularly and frequently to keep the momentum going – every day or every other day. Over time, you might find that you will feel less of a need to write as often. Don't worry if you feel you are repeating yourself, or whether what you are writing down flows or follows a logical thread. Just write whatever comes to your mind, without censoring it.

WHAT IS USEFUL TO WRITE DOWN

I want to you to write down your thoughts, answers and reflections to the exercises in this book. How much you write is up to you, and you might be drawn more to some exercises than others. However, remember that the more you put into each exercise, the more you will get out of it.

You can also write about:

- Your thoughts and feelings about your loss
- How your life has changed since your loss
- What has been most difficult for you
- What you feel scared about in the future
- Memories or dreams related to your loss
- What you feel confused about and the answers you feel you still need

You can also write letters or address what you are writing directly to the person you have lost, or to someone who has caused or contributed to your loss, if you feel there are things you still would like to say, but you never had the chance (or did not wish) to express them directly. People often find that writing letters can be a cathartic experience, which allows them to let go of certain feelings and find new insights. (See chapter 5 for more guidance).

YOUR SOCIAL SUPPORT SYSTEM

If you want to get better and grieve your loss, you will need the support of others. The task of grieving is a big one, and is not meant to be carried by one person alone. Relationships are so important for our wellbeing while we are grieving – more so than at any other time. It is a compelling fact that one of our biggest sources of anxiety and depression – as well as happiness – is directly related to the quality of our relationships.[9]

Everyone is different when it comes to the kind of relationships that nourish us and we feel comfortable being in. What you need for your wellbeing is someone you can trust and feel comfortable with. When you are grieving, feeling vulnerable and not always liking yourself, it is often hard to reach out to others; you might fear you will be unable to deal with any possible rejection or criticism. However, there is probably nothing that helps us more than having someone really listen to us and acknowledge how we feel – it instantly makes us feel more at peace and hopeful. As human beings we have a great need to attach, to be understood and cared for, and our nervous system will instantly calm down when this need is fulfilled.

WHO TO REACH OUT TO

A social support system is vital for you to get through your grieving process, and if you have distanced yourself from your friends and family recently it is now time to work on reconnecting with them. You don't have to reach out to everyone, but identify those you can trust and who you feel would be the right individuals to be part of your current social support system.

When it comes to your family, draw those who you feel you can trust and rely on closer. Some family dynamics are complex, and if your dealings with your family cause you more distress, it's okay to solely depend on friends and other support. At the same time, your recent loss might be a catalyst for improving and repairing family relationships.

What you truly need is for someone to listen to you and empathize with what is going on for you. You deserve someone to be with you and with your painful feelings, who will not try to convince you to feel differently. Sometimes you might ask for advice, but it is your choice who and when you ask.

Likewise, it is good to have people in your support system who can give you valued practical support or are good at keeping you in touch with your current life; for example, people you enjoy doing activities with or who are good at lifting your mood.

EXERCISE
Creating Your Social Support System

1. Write down the names of the individuals who you want to be part of your social support system. They should be people who you feel will, to some degree, help you with your grieving process. They can have different roles in your grieving process: good at

listening, good with practical help, good at helping you stay active, etc. You can have as many as you want in your support system, but I suggest that you have at least two people you feel comfortable talking to about your loss, and at least four in total. Remember, some of them will take bigger or smaller roles in supporting you. We are looking for quality rather than quantity, and to make sure you feel adequately supported in all areas.

2. If you feel that you do not have enough people in your life who can support you, it's important to create a bigger support network. This can be accomplished by reconnecting with old friends, building stronger connections with work colleagues, joining support groups, reaching out to family members, or seeking therapy.

3. Write down any ideas of where you could find more support if needed, and make it a priority to start reaching out. Trying out more than one possible source of support will be useful to ensure that you have different options available; you can then choose the person or source that suits you the best.

MAKING THE MOST OF YOUR SUPPORT SYSTEM

1. The best way to start accessing your support system is by contacting the person you feel will be the easiest to talk to, and who you know will understand and support you. It helps if this person is usually reliable and easy to get hold of on the phone or to meet up with, even if it is only for a short time. Most people will want to help if you are honest about your struggles. Everyone can usually relate to how

desperate it feels to lose someone or something that was very valuable to you.

2. Make a concrete plan of how to reach out to everyone else in your support system. Try to meet with at least one person each week to begin with, and suggest meeting in person rather than speaking on the phone. There is something about real human interaction and being in another person's presence that helps us more than only hearing someone's voice. Of course, if you can only speak on the phone or do so in addition to meeting up, that will be very beneficial, too.

3. Be proactive when reaching out to others – don't wait for others to second-guess what you need. Some people might think you want to be left alone, and fear they will come across as pushy if they suggest keeping in touch or meeting up.

4. Try to reach out to different people at different times, and don't be discouraged if a person is unable to meet you straight away or does not have as much time as you had hoped. Do not take this personally; politely ask if there is another time that suits them. We all have busy lives and you don't know what is happening in their life at the moment – most of the time it does not mean they do not want to meet with you. However, some might find the topic (not you) difficult to deal with. In such cases, respect their decision and move on to someone else.

HOW YOUR SUPPORT SYSTEM CAN HELP YOU

Your support system can help you with a range of things you might be struggling with at the moment, from helping you with practical tasks to keeping you motivated and hopeful. Most importantly, they will help you with dealing with your emotions and processing your grief by listening to you, and sometimes reflecting back what they hear you are saying and how they understand your grief. It's a basic psychological human need to have our emotions acknowledged and validated. Therefore, it is important to talk to those close to you as much as you can – about your feelings, your questions, your confusion and anything else you are finding difficult. Telling the story of your loss can be very powerful, and it will be immensely useful for you to tell your story to as many people as possible. (See chapter 6 for more guidance.)

When you do talk to those in your support network, please bear in mind that in some situations others may not know what to say or how to comfort you. They may even say something that might sound unhelpful or disparaging. Remember, we all get it wrong at times. This usually happens if someone is not clear about what you are feeling. Therefore, your best approach is to never assume that they know how you feel or what is going through your mind. Be direct. Grief is complicated and feelings change, so it is difficult for others to know which stage you are at and what you are feeling today. Say what you find helpful and what you find difficult to relate to. You will then receive more beneficial support, and those around you will thank you for being upfront with them, as they can be more be useful and feel less worried about saying the wrong thing.

CHAPTER SUMMARY

- Good self-care is especially beneficial when you are going through a difficult time emotionally.
- Set up a self-care routine that is realistic and you feel confident you can follow; add and change the routine as you go along if necessary.
- Scheduling in regular grieving time will give you a greater sense of control and will help to contain your feelings and thoughts. It will also help your progress if you set aside time to do activities that help you to process your loss.
- Writing things down helps you to identify and manage your feelings and thought processes, and to realize new insights and ways of viewing your loss.
- Writing down your thoughts, reflections and answers to the exercises in this book will make a huge difference to how beneficial they are to you. Finding a medium that suits your personal style will help you stay motivated to write things down.
- The task of grieving is a big one and needs to be shared – you will need support from others.
- Your support system will help you to deal with your emotions and to process your grief by actively listening to your story, thoughts and emotions. They will also help you with practical tasks, keep you hopeful and less alone, and help you engage with pleasurable activities.

4

WHERE DO YOU WANT TO GET TO?

In this chapter we will look at your personal loss and help you to define where you want to get to – what you are working toward.

Don't worry if you still feel unsure or have doubts about how this is all going to work. It's completely understandable that you might feel this way right now. Loss does not make us feel very hopeful. Bear with me and I will take you through every step, which will be very easy to follow.

You might already have come to the conclusion that you need to face some of those not so nice feelings and memories, and are ready to take the next step, but part of you – or perhaps most of you – might feel some resistance, or worry that things might not get a lot better. Whatever you feel and think right now, there is no right or wrong and we will get you through this.

WHAT TO KEEP IN MIND WHEN DEFINING YOUR GOALS

Before we think about where you want to get to with your grieving process, I want you to keep in mind some common facts about grieving and loss.

GRIEVING CANNOT BE OVERCOME AND SUDDENLY DISAPPEAR ONE DAY

Instead, the raw and intense emotions lessen in intensity and become less frequent until – at some time in the future – you will hardly notice they are there, or you will only be reminded about them occasionally.

Think of an older relative in your family who passed away maybe five or ten years ago – can you remember being upset when they died? Are you still upset to the same extent and as often? Most people find that after some time they have brief moments of remembering the loss and feeling a sudden sadness or yearning, but the feelings and memories are generally very distant.

Sometimes, people stop being upset about their loss altogether, and even when they remember it, they are no longer distressed. Over time, the pain and upset lessens ever more. The loss will always affect you, but once you move through your grief, it will hurt less and less; you might even find invaluable new meaning and insight about yourself, and in your life, through having experienced your loss.

LOSS AND GRIEVING IS PART OF LIFE

Unfortunately, there will always be loss and grief – it is unavoidable. In fact, if you try to limit your life in order to avoid loss, the unintended consequences are that you will lose out in other ways. For example, if you are so fearful of commitment and rejection that you decide to never commit in a relationship again, you will lose out on the possibility of security, companionship, lasting love, a family and a sense of belonging. Life will always be full of awful, uncomfortable and very painful experiences, for all of us. Loss makes up a big part of those experiences. You are not alone in this struggle, and it is just a part of human existence that we need to learn to understand and cope with. Every ending is a new beginning, and what this new beginning will look like lies partly in your hands.

GRIEVING AND HEALING IS AN ACTIVE PROCESS

Grieving and healing will happen naturally if we do not actively try to avoid it. Don't underestimate your intentions about where you would like to get to, or how powerful these intentions can be on a conscious and unconscious level. Our mind always follows a goal or something it believes will benefit us in the long term. However, you might be unaware of what it is your mind is currently trying to achieve; it is therefore very powerful to identify and keep hold of personal, realistic and positive goals going forward.

WHERE DO YOU WANT TO GET TO?

Our minds are fascinating, and usually do an amazing job in helping us to cope, adapt and survive in our challenging world, leading our complex lives. Our minds are programmed to help us heal and recover from any loss, but things can get in the way and make grieving difficult for us. One thing that really helps your mind to process the loss and find the necessary internal resources to grieve is if you let your mind know where you actually want to get to.

You can set your grieving process in motion by giving your mind focus and direction. You can easily get stuck with what you do *not* want, but this can be quite debilitating and does not support your mind to find a way to how you *actually* want to feel about yourself day to day. Holding in mind where you want to get to is to open yourself up to the possibility that things can be different. It will also help your brain to start trying to find solutions to reach the new state. The following technique to help you identify where you want to get to is partly adapted from what has been successfully used in EMDR.

THREE-STEP TECHNIQUE TO HELP YOU IDENTIFY WHERE YOU WANT TO GET TO

Each step is followed by an example of what completing the step would look like.

Step 1: Describe Your Loss(es) in Detail

To help you identify where you want to get to, it is essential to be aware of and able to name all aspects of your loss, and how they affect your current situation. Write down in detail what you have lost. This might feel quite overwhelming to start with, but writing it down will help to contain it. It might also feel like a relief to be able to let it all out, however negative and hopeless it might sound at the moment.

1. Of course, there will be the obvious primary loss, but think about what you have learnt so far and see what else you feel you might have lost as a result of your primary loss. Have you lost other people, parts of your identity, security, or hopes and fantasies? (See page 8.)

2. Write down how things have been different since you have experienced your loss. Has your routine changed? What have you stopped doing or started doing? How have your thoughts changed, and what is your mind focusing on? How has your social life been affected and your close relationships (family, friends, partner)? Do you sleep more or less? Write down anything that feels important to you.

3. What are your main feelings about your loss at the moment?

4. Are there any other previous losses, connected to your current loss, that might be affecting you now? Your recent break-up might be reminding you of your parents separating when you were younger, or your loss of employment and financial security might remind you of your late grandfather, who you always looked up to and

felt safe with while growing up. It is useful to go through the main losses you feel you have experienced throughout your life – however big or small – and see if any of them feel connected to your current loss. If they do, it's important to include these unresolved past losses when working through this book, and address them together with your current loss.

Let's look at an example of how Martin described his loss.

MARTIN'S STORY

I lost the marketing company I founded with my business partner, due to insolvency after the global economic crisis. As I was one of the directors, I also lost my job, my financial security and my lifestyle. My business partner and I always worked well together, and we were friends before we started the business, but I feel after all the difficulties we have been through that I might have lost him as both a friend and trusted business partner.

What hurts me the most is that this company had always been my dream, and I put so much effort and long hours of work into it as I had such high hopes for it, and now I feel it was all for nothing. I have lost a lot of confidence, and am no longer so sure of my capabilities. Even though my wife is supportive, I feel I have let her and my children down – it's as if I have lost my confidence in being a husband and a dad as well, to some degree.

Since it all happened, I have been spending a lot of time in my office at home obsessively going over what happened, trying to analyze it, as well as looking into the future and desperately trying to either find a job or a way to start up another company – even though I do not feel I have the energy right now to ever do this again. I used to run regularly, but I stopped a while ago, and generally feel very tired. I don't really feel like talking to anyone, and find it hard to have my family around me. I know my wife feels stressed about the situation; I try to avoid her as I feel guilty, and I do not have any solutions or anything to say. I think it is easier for me to snap at my family these days, which I am not proud of.

My main feelings about my loss are feeling on edge and anxious. I also feel very low and tired all the time. Sometimes, I get very angry with the situation and the world and why it had to happen, and then I start blaming myself for not seeing it coming.

My dad had his own business, and when I was 12, he also lost his company and we had to move house as my parents were no longer able to afford the mortgage. It was quite a stressful time, and my brother and I even had to move schools. My dad managed to build another successful company, but there were maybe three years when things were quite difficult. I never felt as happy in the place we moved to or at the new school as I had been before.

I am not sure if these are losses that are connected to my current loss, but thinking about it is making me very sad and it triggers a similar feeling of loss of confidence to the feeling I have about losing my business. I think it is probably important to address these losses from my past together with my current loss.

Step 2: Goal 1: Changes You Want to See in Yourself

This step will focus on helping you choose specific and realistic goals of what changes you would like to see in yourself once you have recovered from your loss.

1. Hold in mind how you are feeling at the moment and what is most difficult for you about your current loss and the grieving process.
2. Read through the following list of changes, written as statements in the first person, which indicate that you are showing signs of recovery from your loss (adapted from *How to Go On Living When Someone You Love Dies* by Dr Therese Rando).[10]
3. Choose up to three goals that you haven't fully reached yet, but would like to work toward, and which would make the biggest difference to you.
4. Make a note of your choices and feel free to adapt them if you feel there is a better way to describe where you want to get to.

POSSIBLE SIGNS OF RECOVERY FROM YOUR LOSS

- I have returned to my normal levels of psychological, social, and physical functioning in all realms of my life.
- I am not overwhelmed by strong emotions in general or whenever the loss is mentioned.
- My hatred and anger, if any, doesn't consume me and is not directed inappropriately at others.
- It is not that I don't hurt, but the hurt now is limited, manageable and understood.
- I do not have to obsess about, nor think solely of, my loss or lost person.
- I don't become anxious when I have nothing to do; I don't have to be occupied all the time to be without tension.
- I no longer feel exhausted, burdened or tense all the time.
- I can find some meaning in life.

- I am comfortable with my new identity and the new adjustments I have made to accommodate being without my loss or the person I have lost; while I wouldn't have chosen these changes, I am not fighting them now.
- I can look forward to, and make plans for, the future.
- I do not have to hold on to the pain to have a connection with my deceased loved one.
- I am not inappropriately closed down in my feelings, relationships or approaches to life; for example, I do not overprotect myself or fail to take any risks.

5. Rate on a scale of 1–10 (where 1 means not at all and 10 means completely) to what extent you feel you have already reached this goal.

Let's look at the goals Martin chose and how he rated each of them:

- *I do not have to obsess about, nor think solely of, my losses.* **2/10**
- *I no longer feel exhausted, burdened or wound up all the time.* **3/10**
- *I am comfortable with my new identity and the new adjustments I have made to accommodate being without my loss; while I wouldn't have chosen these changes, I am not fighting them now.* **1/10**

Step 3: Goal 2: Defining the Positive Belief You Would Like to Hold About Yourself

We all hold negative and positive beliefs about ourselves. However, it is the negative ones that cause us to struggle emotionally and which get triggered when we are in distress. We all have core beliefs about ourselves, which underpin our sense of being and influence how we perceive and interpret the world. They are often not readily accessible, and we have to bring them to our awareness.

We usually have a set of persistent core beliefs that developed early in childhood. These particular beliefs will influence how you experience and deal with your loss. Targeting those negative beliefs you have about yourself in relation to the loss will take us to the root of your difficulties, and have a powerful effect on all areas you are struggling with at the moment.

The key is to find which negative belief you hold about yourself in relation to what is most distressing for you about the loss. This is very personal and unique to you. For example, going through a divorce is hugely distressing for most people, but what is most distressing about it can be many different things for different people. It can be a sense of failure, loss of control, powerlessness, hopelessness, abandonment, shame, guilt, intense anger toward the other person. It's therefore important to identify which negative belief the loss triggers in you, to be able to help you focus on dealing with the most distressing aspect of it.

Our goal will be to help you reduce the strength of the negative belief you hold about yourself, and replace it with a corresponding positive belief. Imagine you could have gone through a divorce truly believing afterwards that "you did the best you could" or that "you are valuable/lovable". Can you sense how different the loss of a marriage might feel if you were to hold a positive belief about yourself in comparison to a negative one?

Reducing the strength of your negative belief and increasing the strength of your positive belief is the most important goal I want you to hold on to when working through this book.

To be able to identify the positive belief you would like to hold about yourself, and that will be most meaningful to you, we first need to identify your negative belief.

1. Think about the worst part/moment of your loss; for example, how the actual loss, happened, or something that happened before the loss, or the consequences of your loss. Hold in mind whatever causes you the most distress.
2. Think about which **negative** belief you hold about yourself when you think of the worst part/moment of your loss. Have a look through the list of negative beliefs in the table opposite, and pick whichever resonates most with you.
3. Think about the worst part/moment of the loss, and rate on a scale of 0–10 (where 0 means no disturbance at all and 10 means the most disturbance you can imagine) how disturbing it feels now to think of the worst part/moment of your loss and the negative belief about yourself.
4. Think about what **positive** belief you would like to hold about yourself when thinking about your loss. Find the corresponding positive belief to your negative belief in the table below. If there is more than one corresponding positive belief to your negative belief, pick the one that describes best what you would like to believe about yourself. Adjust the wording of the belief if needed.
5. Think about your loss, and rate on a scale of 1-10 (where 1 means not true at all and 10 means completely true) how true the positive statement feels to you right now.

The importance is on how you feel; that is, do not rate it in terms of what you *think* is true, but how true it *feels*.

This is crucial, as you might *know* that your positive belief is true, but if you do not *feel* it then you do not really *believe* it and it won't change how you feel about yourself. For example, you might know that "you did the best you could", as you have the facts and others have told you so, but if you do not feel/believe it on an emotional level, then there is still more grieving and processing left to do.

LIST OF NEGATIVE AND POSITIVE BELIEFS

NEGATIVE BELIEFS	POSITIVE BELIEFS
Self-defectiveness	
I am not good enough	I am good enough
I am a bad person	I am a good/lovable person
I don't deserve love	I deserve love
I am not lovable	I am lovable
I am inadequate	I am adequate
I am worthless/inadequate	I have value/I am valuable
	I am worthy/worthwhile
I am empty/not enough	I am complete/whole
I am weak	I am strong
I am permanently damaged	I am healthy (or can be)
	It is possible for me to find meaning again in my life
I am shameful	I am honourable
	I am fine/okay just the way I am
I am ugly/repulsive	I am fine/attractive/lovable/desirable
I do not deserve...	I deserve/can have...
I am stupid	I am intelligent/competent
I am insignificant/unimportant	I am significant/important/valued
I am a disappointment	I am okay just the way I am
I deserve to be miserable	I deserve to be happy
I am different/don't belong	I am okay as I am
I cannot cope/I cannot handle it	I can cope/I can handle it
	It might take time, but I will always manage
	It is possible to find meaning again in my life

NEGATIVE BELIEFS	POSITIVE BELIEFS
Responsibility	
I should have done something (I am bad)	I did the best I could
I should have known better	I do the best I can (I can learn to do better)
I should have done more	I did my best
I did something wrong (I am bad)	I learned (can learn) from it
It is my fault (I am bad)	I did my best
Safety/Vulnerability	
I am not safe	I am safe now
I am alone	There are people I can trust and who will protect me/care for me
I cannot trust anyone	I can choose who to trust
I am in danger	It's over, I am safe now
I cannot protect myself	I can (learn to) protect myself now and in the future
It is not okay (safe) to feel or show my emotions	I can safely feel and show my emotions
Control/Choice	
I am not in control	I am in control now
I am powerless/I am helpless	I am in control now
	I have choices now
	I am resourceful
I am weak	I am strong
I cannot be trusted	I can be trusted
I cannot trust myself	I can trust myself (or learn to)
I am a failure	I am a success/I can succeed
I am/my situation is hopeless	Other people have gone on to enjoy their life again and so can I
	It is possible for me to be happy again in a different way

Be careful to choose a *belief* from the list and not a *feeling*. For example, "I am sad" would be a correct statement, but it describes how you feel, not what you believe about yourself. In this example, to help you get to the belief, you can ask yourself, "What does being sad say about me? That it is my fault, I am weak...".

Let's look at which negative and positive belief Martin identified for himself in relation to what is most distressing to him about his loss, and how he rated each.

> **Worst part/moment of the loss:** *The moment I realized that our company was going under. We were working late one night (yet again) when my business partner and I finally realized that there was no way we could save our company. It suddenly sunk in what was about to follow, and I felt dreadful about how our employees, customers and my family would be affected.*
> **Negative belief:** *I am a disappointment.* **8/10**
> **Positive belief:** *I am okay just the way I am.* **2/10**

YOUR PERSONAL GOALS AND PROGRESS SO FAR

You should now have a detailed description of your loss, and up to three rated goals from step 2 (page 50). You should have also identified and rated both a positive belief and a negative belief about yourself.

Please make a note of these in the box that follows, or somewhere where you can find them easily. Make sure you date your current ratings. We will periodically go back to them and track whether there have been any changes.

TRACKING YOUR GOALS AND PROGRESS

Date:

Rate on a scale of 1–10 to what extent you feel you have already reached these goals, where 1 means not at all and 10 means completely:

My first goal is: _____

Rating: /10

My second goal is: _____

Rating: /10

My third goal is: _____

Rating: /10

Negative belief: _____

Right now, how disturbing does it feel to think of the worst part/moment of your loss and the negative belief about yourself? Rate on a scale of 0–10, where 0 means no disturbance at all and 10 means the most disturbance you can imagine.

Rating: /10

Positive belief: _____

How true does the positive statement feel to you right now, when you think about your loss? Rate on a scale of 1–10, where 1 means not true at all and 10 means completely true.

Rating: /10

CHAPTER SUMMARY

- Grief cannot suddenly disappear one day. Instead, the raw and intense emotions gradually lessen in intensity and become less frequent.
- Loss and grieving are part of life.
- Defining and engaging with your goals helps you to process your loss and find your necessary internal resources; it also gives your mind focus and direction.
- We all have core (negative and positive) beliefs about ourselves, which underpin our sense of being and influence how we perceive and interpret the world.
- Targeting the negative belief and increasing the positive belief you have about yourself in relation to your loss will take you to the root of your difficulties, and can have a powerful effect on all areas you are struggling with at the moment.
- Rating your goals at the end of each chapter will help you track your progress and keep you motivated.

5

ACCEPTANCE

Acceptance is one of the most important, but also one of the most difficult skills we need to develop and nurture in our life in order to be able to deal with any difficulties. Acceptance does not mean giving in, rather it means *accepting what we cannot change in a given moment, and accepting the pain and discomfort that follows*. In the long term, acceptance significantly lessens the pain and discomfort of your emotions and hence leads to less suffering and struggle.

In this chapter we will look at why acceptance is so important, why acceptance can be difficult and, finally, how to be more accepting. There will be useful exercises for you to do, to help you start becoming more accepting of your emotions and, eventually, your loss.

Acceptance is an essential first step in grieving, and will enable you to move through your grief and move on with your life. In fact, psychotherapists and psychologists have found that people who can accept their thoughts and emotions, rather than fight them, generally find it easier to recover from difficulties, such as suffering a loss, and have better psychological health.[11]

To help you with your grieving process, we need to develop your ability to accept your thoughts and feelings, as well as to accept your loss. Acceptance will help you to end the struggle of fighting a battle you cannot win, and is essential in helping you to get unstuck and move forward.

WHY ACCEPTANCE IS SO IMPORTANT

When we find ourselves in a situation that we do not like as it creates discomfort, we often try our best to reject, deny or avoid whatever makes us feel uncomfortable. This might give us relief in the short term, but it does not resolve anything; in the long term it can cause much bigger problems, and often keeps us stuck and feeling powerless. Rejecting, denying or avoiding uses a lot of effort to give us the impression that something is not as bad as it actually is. We will also always come back to the same feelings, and we will have to expend more energy to keep denying and avoiding what we fear.

Not engaging with your emotions means that your grieving process can never fully happen; and while you might have become very good at pushing those feelings away, they will always stay close to the surface. For example, if you are getting really upset about your loss and feel like crying, then – in this very moment – you cannot change the fact that you feel terribly sad. Telling yourself that you have no reason to be so upset, or "weak", is not going to change the fact that you feel sad. If you reject, deny or avoid your sadness, you will be using a great deal of energy to push the sadness away, and you will have to continue to use this energy to keep it there. This can be exhausting, and, as well as feeling sad, you will start to feel tired and perhaps depressed. You might even become dependent on drugs or alcohol to keep those feelings down; or you might not be able to get close to others out of fear they might say or do something that will trigger the sadness that you are desperately trying to avoid.

Instead, if you accept your sadness, you may well feel a wave of emotion and you are likely to cry, but your sadness will run its course; afterwards, you will feel lighter and you will not have to spend any energy on trying to avoid or deny it. Of course, the same emotion might come back in a different situation or at a later stage, but every time it will be less intense, and you will no longer fear the emotion as you will have learnt how to be with it.

While you might think that denying or rejecting certain emotions keeps you in control, the opposite is actually true. By constantly having to work hard to control and avoid your emotions, they start to control you, and you can never feel completely at peace. Instead, by accepting your thoughts and feelings, you ultimately learn to control them. It is ending the struggle that you cannot win and learning that you can be with and cope with your emotions, however big they are. You might have heard the saying, "Pain is inevitable, but suffering is optional." The pain you feel for your loss is inevitable, but the suffering you create by *not* accepting your pain and your loss is optional.

By allowing yourself to feel your difficult emotions, you are helping yourself to stay in touch with your positive emotions. The more you open up to the sadness, anger, guilt and anxiety without trying to fight against it, the easier it will be for you to experience happiness, contentment and excitement again. Our minds work in an all or nothing approach – we cannot selectively suppress some emotions, but stay in touch with others. Therefore, if you avoid and push away any difficult emotions, I can guarantee you that the positive emotions you crave will also be gone. In the end, this can make you feel like you are just surviving, rather than living. Long-term suppression of your feelings can even contribute to mental illness.

Acceptance is the best tool you have to work against suppression and avoidance of emotions.

WHAT MAKES ACCEPTANCE SO DIFFICULT?

I want to take you through some of the reasons we find it so difficult to accept our emotions and our loss. This should help you make sense of your difficulties and become more understanding of yourself, as well as helping you identify how to challenge some of your perceptions and beliefs about your emotions.

YOUR BELIEFS ABOUT EMOTIONS

How you view emotions, and how easily you accept them, depends largely on what you have learnt from your parents or caregivers when growing up, and how they managed their emotions and dealt with loss. You learn early on how much emotion – and which emotions – are acceptable, and when to suppress or avoid them. Suppressing emotions often leads us to have "emotions about emotions". For example, you might feel sad, but because you have learnt that this means "being weak" and that you should never be weak, you then feel ashamed for feeling sad. When emotions that are not acceptable quickly get replaced by secondary emotions, the initial emotion is not properly felt or moved through, and thus remains unresolved. To truly grieve and heal from your loss, all emotions need to be accepted and felt.

SOCIAL INFLUENCES

From a social perspective, depending on the country and culture you grew up in, you might have been socialized into suppressing your emotions. In many societies, there is often no time and space for feeling and expressing emotions, as we constantly strive for achievement. Young children are naturally much better at expressing and fully feeling emotions, and better at moving on from them as quickly as they arose. Observe a toddler – it is fascinating how strongly they can feel something and express their feeling with their whole body, yet they never seem to hold on to their emotions for a long time. Of course, young children do not have the capacity to control and manage emotions, which can lead to other problems and huge frustrations. However, it's important to remember that, as we grow up, we somehow lose the skill to fully be with our feelings and move through them. We quickly learn that our society overtly values suppressing and controlling emotions, which can make it difficult for us to feel comfortable with them. It can lead to not learning how to cope with our feelings apart from suppressing them, which is never successful.

FEAR OF LOSING CONTROL

Many people are fearful of accepting their thoughts and emotions as they worry about losing control or that their emotions will become overwhelmingly strong and unmanageable. In the moment, they also fear that the feelings will last forever and get increasingly worse if they do not stop them.

WHAT ACTUALLY HAPPENS WHEN YOU ACCEPT YOUR EMOTIONS?

While accepting your emotions will make you feel them more strongly to begin with, their intensity will lessen soon after and you will be able to cope with them.

The reason why the strength of your emotions will soon reduce is that our state of mind is never permanent – it changes all the time. Your mind is not able to hold on to the same emotion at the same intensity for long periods of time, rather it focuses on different thoughts and experiences every second.

Take a moment, and reflect on how you have been feeling today so far. I am pretty sure that the way you felt this morning will be different to how you feel right now. You might have felt very tired and hopeless this morning, but then felt completely different when you went out for a walk; and you will again be feeling differently, reading this book right now. However bad you feel, remind yourself that all feelings pass eventually. They might come back, but they will not last forever.

If you choose to stay with a strong emotion rather than suppress it, the intensity will never last, as your mind will be able to understand and process what is happening/has happened and start to see things from a different perspective. The better your mind can make sense of what is happening/has happened and see it in a more balanced way, the less overwhelming and unmanageable the emotion or memory will feel. To enable your mind to see a situation differently, you need to allow it to stay with the emotion or memory for long enough. Your mind will only be able to find a different solution or perspective if you allow it enough time to work it out! It's a bit like trying to solve a maths problem by only looking at it for a split second and then looking away, because it feels too difficult and you panic. What you need to do is to look at it long enough, and feel the discomfort and confusion, until you finally find a pattern or a solution.

To illustrate the two points above, let's assume that you get really upset about remembering when your ex-boyfriend left your apartment after you had broken up. The more you think about the memory while fully accepting that it happened and how you feel about it, the less intense your emotions will become as time passes. You will probably feel very sad and you might cry a lot to begin with, but with time you won't get overwhelmed by your sadness. You will have allowed your mind to look at the memory and the connected feelings for long enough to see it from different perspectives, re-assess what else might have been going on, how it came about, the range of feelings you have toward your ex-boyfriend and how you understand the situation now, etc. That will allow you to process what has happened. You will end up having a more balanced and realistic, rather than overwhelming and one-sided, view of the break-up. Once you have fully accepted and processed the feeling, you will feel lighter and calmer. It will likely still not be a very nice memory, but your sadness will be a lot less than it was to begin with.

It's really important for you to set aside your grief time and learn to accept and be with your emotions, so they don't take over the rest of your life.

HOW TO BE MORE ACCEPTING

In order to value yourself and honour the loss you experienced, make sure you give it all the time and space it needs. Learning to accept your thoughts, emotions and your loss is a skill that will serve you all your life and can transform how you experience yourself and how you cope with difficulties.

Let's look at what acceptance looks like in practice, and what will help you to expand your acceptance.

IDENTIFYING FEELINGS

Sometimes the first hurdle to acceptance is being unable to identify the emotion you are feeling, especially if you have secondary emotions or feel uncomfortable about an emotion. You might notice "not liking something" or feeling a bit on edge, but it might be hard to pinpoint what is causing this. The exercise that follows will help you identify your feelings.

Let's go back to the previous example to illustrate what it might look like when you struggle to identify a feeling. Let's assume friends ask you how you are feeling and if you are doing okay after your break-up, but you do not want to talk about it.

The feeling you experience may be anger toward the people who have asked how you are. If people are being nosy or pushy you have every reason to feel angry, but you might also have a feeling that there is more to this emotion. When you ask yourself what you might be finding so hard about friends asking how you are, you realize that you are still struggling with the break-up, and you do not want to tell them this. Again, asking why this might be the case, you realize that you don't want to come across as someone who is always down; you fear that your friends will get tired of you and you will end up even lonelier. This makes you feel very sad and anxious, too. The feelings that need attention and acceptance in this example are, therefore, anger, sadness and anxiety. As you can see, it's sometimes not clear to start with what we are feeling, and we sometimes need to reflect and do some detective work to identify which feelings need accepting.

EXERCISE
Identifying Feelings

Use this exercise when you struggle to identify what you are feeling, or think that there might be some feelings you are not aware of.

1. Identify the thought you have when you think of a particular memory/aspect related to your loss: "I don't like X."
   Example: I don't like it when my friends ask how I am.
2. Ask yourself, "What is so bad about X?" Your answer will be, "X is so bad because of Y."
   Example: What's bad about my friends asking me, is that I still struggle with the break-up and I don't want to share this.

3. Ask yourself, "What is so bad about Y?" Your answer will be: "Y is so bad because of Z." Repeat this questioning until you come to a conclusion about what it is that makes you feel so uncomfortable about the memory/aspect.

   Example: What's so bad about telling them that I still struggle is that I do not want to come across as someone who is always down. What's so bad about being depressed is that I fear I will lose my friends and I will end up even lonelier.

4. Identify what you feel about your concluding statement.

   Example: I feel very sad and anxious.

EXERCISE
Identifying and Accepting the Feelings You are Not Comfortable With

1. Spend some time thinking about your loss and the feelings you do not feel comfortable with. They will likely be the ones you want to turn away from or suppress instantly, or the ones that make you cringe or do something to distract yourself from. Think about moments over the past week when you were overcome by unpleasant feelings that you did not want to accept.

   Example: Remembering how my ex-boyfriend would make "funny" comments about me being boring. I don't like to remember those moments now as they make me feel ashamed of myself and worthless.

2. When you notice an uncomfortable feeling, notice the feeling, name the feeling and normalize it. Make a note of the feeling.
   Example: I am feeling shame.

3. Be curious about what it is about that feeling you find hard to accept. Write down whatever comes to your mind. Let yourself fully feel the emotion, and let it expand as much as it wants to; resist the urge to change it or get rid of it.
   Example: The shame feels horrible and makes me want to hide from everyone. It feels awful to think that perhaps everyone finds me boring. Feeling utterly worthless feels so overpowering – like there is nothing I can change, and I just have to put up with feeling awful about myself.

4. Then say to yourself, "I can learn to accept and cope with feeling X. Other people are able to do this, and so am I." Just sit with how that feels. Don't worry if you don't completely believe the statement, just allow the possibility that this could be true.

5. Either make a note to further work on becoming more accepting of this particular feeling at a later stage, or go straight to the next exercise: "Expanding acceptance of your emotions", using the identified feeling. Move on to the next feeling you feel uncomfortable with and repeat steps 1 to 4.

Using this approach to practise identification and acceptance of your emotions will help in the following way:

- Communicating a feeling clearly to yourself (and others) helps with regulating your emotions and makes them more manageable.

- Acknowledging your feelings helps you to realize that you and your feelings matter, and that you have the patience and willingness to fully accept yourself, which is very soothing.
- Giving a feeling (or sensation) that is overwhelming a name will help you to feel more in control, as you now know what you are dealing with; it is no longer a chaos of sensations in your body mixed in with lots of thoughts and images, but a distinct feeling you can work with.

Don't judge your feelings, and be aware when experiencing secondary feelings; for example, feeling guilty about feeling sad. Both feelings are valid and deserve attention. Don't feel you need to take action or resolve this feeling at this point.

To help you with accepting your emotions and thoughts, be curious. Be curious about your feelings, about yourself, about what happens if you just allow your feelings to be, and about how your complicated yet fascinating human mind works. Open up, give yourself permission, be willing and release the struggle. Accepting does not mean giving in or giving up, but accepting what is and what needs to happen.

  After some time, you will notice that – by not trying to change anything at all – how you feel about your loss and yourself is changing, anyway.

EXERCISE
Expanding Acceptance of Your Emotions

Find a place where you will not be disturbed and where you feel comfortable. You can close your eyes if you wish to.

1. Identify how you are feeling about your loss at this moment in time, using the previous exercise if you struggle with identifying what you are feeling. If there are several feelings, start with the strongest one.

2. Acknowledge that this is how you are feeling in this very moment. You do not need to change it.

3. Rate how strongly you feel the feeling from 0 to 10, with 10 being the strongest.

4. Name the feeling and normalize it. Tell yourself that it is understandable that you feel this way in your situation, and that it is not easy to experience this emotion. Remind yourself that the feeling won't last and it will pass.

5. Notice where the feeling is in your body, and describe it to yourself while paying attention to those body parts. Does the feeling feel heavy, tight, painful, hot, like an electric current, empty, like a knot, nauseating, like a wave, like you want to cry, etc.? Once you have identified the feeling in your body, pay attention to it for a couple of minutes and just observe it without trying to change it. Be mindful not to get distracted by thoughts, and stay with the sensation.

6. What would the feeling make you do if you allowed it to fully express itself? Cry, hide away, shout, collapse, be aggressive, run away, hug someone, etc.? Imagine actually doing that action. Remember that it is your

imagination, and that you are allowed to do or imagine whatever you wish as long as it feels safe. If necessary, try imagining different things until you feel that you have completely expressed your feeling.

7. Notice what you are feeling in your body now, and rate the strength of feeling from 0 to 10.

8. The intensity of your feeling will most likely have decreased, but if not, do not worry – it only means that your feeling requires more attention and more acceptance. If you wish, you can give the feeling more attention until it has decreased further.

9. Make some notes in your journal about what you have been feeling. What have you learnt from this exercise? What was difficult/easy? What was helpful? What have you learnt about the feeling you were working with? Did you gain any insights? What surprised you, if anything?

Generally, this exercise is absolutely fine to use and very effective. However, there are certain circumstances when you will trigger an emotion that is too distressing (often connected to a traumatic memory), which will mean that the intensity of feeling will still be high at the end of the exercise, or that you will be unable to complete the exercise due to feeling too overwhelmed. If this is the case, and you are finding it difficult to carry on with your day-to-day tasks, carry out some grounding exercises.

1. Get up and walk around, being aware of your feet touching the ground.

2. Look around yourself and name objects inside your room or outside the window.

3. Tell yourself which day of the week and which month it is.

4. Tell yourself where you are right now – building/place/ city/country.
5. Smell a perfume or an aromatherapy oil (strong smells work better).
6. Make yourself a hot or cold drink.

These grounding exercises will help you orient yourself in the present and get you in touch with the here and now in both mind and body. Repeat the grounding exercises until you feel better.

It's normal to feel overwhelmed by emotions sometimes and to be unable to practise acceptance straight away. However, if you are concerned about the intensity of your emotions, or if engaging with certain emotions is making you feel spaced out or disconnected, I suggest you seek external help from a qualified therapist as it might be difficult for you to work through this book on your own (see chapter 9).

EXERCISE
Writing a Letter to Your Loss

This exercise will help you to get in touch with some of the feelings you have about your loss and accepting those feelings. This, in turn, will help you with developing acceptance of your loss.

Make sure you allocate at least 20 to 30 minutes for this exercise so you have enough time to reflect on what you have written and to practise accepting the feelings that will have arisen. Make sure you feel safe and comfortable before starting to write the letter.

You can write the letter in any format you like, but these are some of the themes and topics you might want to cover. Fill in the blanks from your own experience.

Dear ...

I have really struggled since I lost you. I miss so many things about you..., which has made me feel...
Since I have lost you, I have been... and my life has been... [Write what you have been doing and how all aspects of your life have been different since your loss; include both positives and negatives.]

The most upsetting memory I have about you is... [Write which memory you find most upsetting now; it can be from before or after the loss, or the actual loss], which makes me feel...
The nicest memory I have about you is..., which makes me feel...

What I really want you to know/wanted to say to you is...
What I would like to leave behind is... [Write about which aspect of the loss or what/who you have lost that you would like to leave behind and move on from.]
What I most value about having had you in my life/The most important thing you taught me is...

Saying goodbye and accepting that you have gone is making me feel...
And I hope that in the future I will feel... and remember you as...

Once you have written your letter, decide what you would like to do with it. Some people like to keep it as it captures how they feel about their loss, others like to get rid to symbolize letting go of the loss. Do whatever is right for you and has meaning to you.

REVIEWING YOUR GOALS AND BELIEFS ABOUT YOURSELF

Please take as much time as you need to complete the exercises in this chapter. Practising acceptance of your emotions is something that takes a while to feel comfortable with, and needs to become something you do regularly to be effective. It is to be expected that some of the exercises will be difficult and make you very emotional, and it is important to look after yourself and your needs. There is no rush – be patient, kind and supportive toward yourself, and take one step at a time.

Once you have completed all the exercises, update the ratings of your goals and the beliefs about yourself in relation to your loss, which you identified in the last chapter. Don't worry if they still haven't shifted very much or have shifted in the opposite direction to the one you were hoping for. Opening up to difficult feelings and experiences can feel like things are getting worse to start with. If your ratings are getting "worse", it may be because when you initially rated your goals and beliefs you were not completely in touch with how difficult things have been for you. Accepting and being with your emotions will therefore feel like they are stronger and worse, but they are actually the same – you are just no longer suppressing or avoiding them.

You are doing really well – you are learning to be with these difficult feelings and soon they will no longer be able to control you or keep you stuck, and they *will* become less intense.

If you are seeing some change in the right direction, make sure to acknowledge to yourself how well you have already done in working through your grief, regardless of how small or big the change is. Every change is important and, step by step, you will get there.

TRACKING YOUR GOALS AND PROGRESS

Date:

Rate on a scale of 1–10 to what extent you feel you have already reached these goals, where 1 means not at all and 10 means completely:

My first goal is: _____
Rating: /10
My second goal is: _____
Rating: /10
My third goal is: _____
Rating: /10

Negative belief: _____
Right now, how disturbing does it feel to think of the worst part/moment of your loss and the negative belief about yourself? Rate on a scale of 0–10, where 0 means no disturbance at all and 10 means the most disturbance you can imagine.
Rating: /10

Positive belief: _____
How true does the positive statement feel to you right now when you think about your loss? Rate on a scale of 1–10, where 1 means not true at all and 10 means completely true.
Rating: /10

CHAPTER SUMMARY

- Acceptance will help you to get unstuck and move forward.
- Rejecting, denying, avoiding or suppressing emotions is a short-term solution that leads to more intense and overwhelming emotions in the long term.
- Suppressing difficult emotions leads to suppression of positive and enjoyable emotions.
- Beliefs about emotions, social influences, and fears about emotions can make acceptance difficult.
- Accepting your emotions will make you feel them more strongly to begin with, but their intensity will lessen and you will be able to cope with them.
- Acceptance helps with regulating your emotions and making you feel more in control.
- Learning to identify your emotions is an important first step in learning to accept your emotions.
- In a nutshell, you can practise accepting your emotions by identifying/naming the feeling, noticing the feeling in your body, and acknowledging that this is how you are feeling in this moment, without trying to change or avoid it.
- Practising accepting your emotions takes a while to feel comfortable with, and needs to be done regularly to be effective.

6

UNDERSTANDING YOUR LOSS

Understanding your loss entails remembering your loss and identifying what it means to you. Depending on who or what you have lost, it might seem fairly obvious to you why it is affecting you so deeply. However, there might be a time or moments when you question why it is (still) causing you so much upset. I will help you to develop a better understanding of your loss through creating a timeline of the events surrounding your loss and writing your personal story. We will also look at your previous experiences of grief and how they might still be influencing you now.

THE VALUE OF UNDERSTANDING YOUR LOSS

Understanding your loss is a way of making sense of all the chaos and creating order in your own mind. Understanding in detail what is causing your strong emotional responses, and linking it to your other relevant life experiences, will help you make sense of what is going on. Once you understand and acknowledge the meaning of your loss, and you are able to see the bigger picture, it will be easier for you to come to terms with it and cope with your emotions.

An important element in supporting your understanding will be to remember the details that led to your loss, your actual loss and what has happened since. Remembering those details will help you to develop a realistic and balanced memory. You can only fully process and move on from an experience in your life that you have made sense of and that you can reflect on in realistic terms; therefore, your loss needs to be remembered and acknowledged as a coherent and balanced story.

FACTORS THAT AFFECT THE IMPACT OF YOUR LOSS

Each loss is unique and will have a unique meaning to you. Sometimes we can get lost in the pain and emotional turmoil we experience when we are grieving, and it becomes difficult to see the bigger picture. Understanding which factors of your loss contribute to the loss's impact on you can help you make sense of your strong emotions and put things into perspective.

Some of these factors might mean that the grieving process is more difficult for you compared to someone else in a similar situation. Remember that none of the factors are your fault, but are a result of the circumstances you are in. You might be able to address some of the factors, while others might be out of your control.

The impact of your loss is determined by a variety of factors, and we will look at the predominant ones to help you better understand your loss. Keep your loss in mind while reading through the different factors below, and notice which details are relevant to you. You can either make notes while you read through the list or complete the exercise at the end of this section.

The seven predominant factors that can affect the impact of your loss are:

1. The negative core belief your loss triggers in you
2. The significance of your loss
3. The nature of your loss
4. Unresolved issues and mixed feelings about the person you have lost
5. A lack of practical and emotional support
6. Other life stressors
7. Previous losses

THE NEGATIVE CORE BELIEF YOUR LOSS TRIGGERS IN YOU

Take a moment to remind yourself of the negative belief you hold about yourself in relation to your loss, which we identified in chapter 4. The reason that your loss is so painful and difficult to process is that it has triggered this core belief in yourself.

This negative belief is probably one that causes you a lot of distress and is likely to be a familiar feeling, given that it has been present for much of your life. The fact that your loss has triggered this entrenched negative belief makes it harder to move on from the loss. If you believe that you are "worthless" and then experience the loss of a relationship you valued, you may feel you did not deserve the relationship in the first place. This will be very upsetting as you might have felt that the relationship gave you worth; losing that relationship makes you think that you will just have to accept this negative belief. If you believe this strongly, you will probably feel quite depressed. Alternatively, the loss of a relationship might make you feel that you are "powerless" as however hard you tried, you could not save the relationship. In turn you now feel anxious and low about any future relationships, as you don't believe you could ever make any relationship last.

It is completely understandable that your experience of loss can strengthen negative beliefs about yourself. You could probably give examples that "prove" that your belief is true – comments others have made to you, or what you perceive happens to other people in your situation, or how you feel you have been treated. Maybe the most unshakeable evidence you have is that you just feel your negative belief so strongly that there can be no other conclusion other than it must be true. If we were to accept all of the above, then it is no wonder that your loss feels so overwhelming and difficult to work through. However, it is slightly more complex than this.

The difficulty with core beliefs is that we often do our best, unconsciously, to find evidence that our core beliefs are true. This is why the same experience will trouble different people in different ways. We unconsciously pay attention to all the evidence that supports our core beliefs, and disregard anything that will challenge them. This is why it is so important to think about what positive core belief you would like to hold about yourself instead; opening yourself up to the possibility that you could believe this about yourself will help you become more open to recognizing and noticing evidence and details that support your positive belief. We are not trying to change the belief you have about yourself by convincing you to believe something different; we are helping you to see things in a more realistic way, which will help you to find and see the supportive evidence that your positive belief is true.

To summarize – one reason why your loss feels so awful is because it has triggered your negative core belief(s). One way of addressing your current difficulties and helping you with your grief is to help you weaken your negative core belief(s) and strengthen your positive core belief(s). You will achieve this by following the exercises in this book and by reviewing your negative and positive beliefs at the end of each chapter.

THE SIGNIFICANCE OF YOUR LOSS

The more important the person or what you have lost was to you, the bigger the impact your loss will have on you. The closer we are to someone and the longer we have known them for are just as important as how crucial someone or something is for our survival and meeting our basic needs. What you have lost might have been an integral part of your identity. For example, if your profession and the life that comes with it is an important part of who you are and/or a major source of your self-esteem, losing your job is likely to hit you very hard.

THE NATURE OF YOUR LOSS

How your loss occurred and the events around it will affect how easy or difficult it might be for you to come to terms with it and make sense of it.

It is usually easier for us to grieve a loss when it was somewhat predictable and we had time to prepare ourselves to some degree. It will also make it easier for you if the loss happened in as calm a way as possible, and you felt a sense of agency and control. But if your loss was sudden and unpredictable, you may be in shock for quite some time. If you felt powerless and out of control about the loss or while it was happening, that can add significant distress

Of course, nothing can really prepare you for how you will feel and what is going to happen when your loss actually happens.

Let's assume you are estranged from your father as he suddenly walked out one day after a violent row with your mother. You never fully understood why it happened, nor saw it coming. As such, it will be much harder for you to come to terms with this than if you had experienced a calm and planned separation. Although the planned separation might have led to you becoming estranged from your father nevertheless, you may have felt more in control of that choice.

How your loss came about is significant in that it affects us differently depending on what we believe caused the loss. Your loss will be particularly distressing if it was deliberately caused by another person; for example, when someone is murdered, or if you became disabled due to an accident involving a drunk driver. This might leave you feeling that the loss could have been avoided, and that all your suffering is due to the negligence or wilful wrongdoing of another. It is usually slightly easier for us to accept things that happen without anyone else's involvement, or if we feel that we had a degree of control or choice in what was happening.

How the loss occurred is also important. If your loss was very graphic or horrific, you will suffer a great deal more than if it was something that you are likely to experience at some point in your life. Losing a family member to death by suicide is an experience most will find very difficult to deal with. Whereas experiencing the death of a family member in a hospice where they have been cared for with dignity and respect is easier to process and move on from.

Please bear in mind that your initial emotions and shock might be considerably stronger depending on the nature of your loss. Therefore, to start with, you might need more time for yourself and more support to deal with the shock and the overwhelming feelings. If the nature of your loss was horrific, sudden and has left you feeling out of control and powerless, you might even experience symptoms of trauma. If you do have concerns about trauma, please refer to chapter 9 to find out whether it would be advisable for you to seek additional help.

UNRESOLVED ISSUES AND MIXED FEELINGS

If you are grieving the loss of a person in your life – either through death, the break-up of a relationship, or estrangement – the grieving process is usually more complex when you have mixed feelings or unresolved issues with the one you have lost. Coming to the realization that one will never have a chance to resolve these issues might make you feel you will never be able to change the feelings you had and now have, and to find closure.

Losing someone we generally only have negative or mixed feelings toward adds to the emotional turmoil we have already felt about this person. You might feel completely overwhelmed from trying to work things through after all the pain they have caused you, and find it hard to come to a place where you feel largely at peace with it all and can leave things behind. We look at helping you to make peace with difficult relationships and deal with "unfinished business" in chapters 10 and 11.

LACK OF SUPPORT

Having available – and making use of – plentiful and quality practical and emotional support when you experience your loss will make it easier for you to get through the first difficult stages of your grieving process. When we feel so vulnerable and unable to think clearly, or sometimes even unable to look after ourselves, we need others to make sure we are okay and to listen to our story and struggles.

It makes a huge difference if you feel you have someone you can trust and openly talk to about your experiences and concerns. Later during your grieving, you will need others not only to share how you are feeling, but also to help you get back to your normal life again and to help you when you feel stuck, not only emotionally, but also practically. The support you will need will be different depending on your loss and your personality, and might include emotional, financial, practical, psychological, medical or spiritual support.

Not having anyone to adequately support you emotionally and practically can make the grieving process so much more difficult. See chapter 3 for help with how to set up a social support system.

OTHER LIFE STRESSORS

Grieving takes a lot of energy and resources, and it will be even more demanding if you have other difficulties to deal with at the same time. You might be contending with relationship problems, family problems, illness, problems at work or financial difficulties at the same time as you are grieving. These might hold you back from allocating enough time and energy to working through your loss.

Specifically, if you already have a mental health illness, such as an anxiety disorder or depression, or if you suffer from severe low self-esteem, you will find it more difficult to grieve. Grief will be an extra weight on top of your ongoing struggles with your mental health, and might make your mental illness worse for some time.

All the exercises and insights in this book will be relevant to you and will help you with your grieving as well as with any other life stressors. Please keep in mind that understandably you might need more time and external support to help you with all your current difficulties. There is advice and guidance regarding how to identify whether you have a mental health disorder and when to seek help, in chapter 9.

PREVIOUS LOSSES

Finally, let's consider how previous losses affect how easy or difficult it is for you to grieve the loss you want to work through at the moment. Most of us carry around unresolved and maybe even unacknowledged losses, which leave us emotionally vulnerable when it comes to grieving – the unresolved feelings and thoughts from the past are triggered in addition to our current feelings, leaving us overwhelmed. Only if you deal with your past loss, will you be fully able to address your current loss. Therefore, it is important to become aware of any past losses that are still affecting you, and to address them alongside your most recent loss. This might seem quite overwhelming at first, but, as discussed in chapter 4, being aware of which losses are still affecting you will help you to make better sense of what you are going through at the moment, and to find resolution. Whilst working through this book, always keep your most recent loss – as well as any previous losses – in mind to ensure you will make the progress you are looking for.

EXERCISE
Factors that Affect the Impact of My Loss

Go through each of the seven factors listed, and make a note of any details you feel are relevant about your loss for each section.

Below are some examples completed by Sophia, who had a late miscarriage when she was 19 weeks pregnant.

1. The negative core belief your loss triggers in you.
   I am worthless.
2. The significance of your loss.
   Being/becoming a mum has always been a huge part of my identity. I fear that I might have to let go of that part and that there will be nothing to fill the void.
3. The nature of your loss.
   The loss was very unexpected as the first scan was all fine. The miscarriage itself was a horrible ordeal to have to go through – especially being induced and giving birth to Lisa after she had died.
4. Unresolved issues and mixed feelings about the person you have lost.
   None.
5. Lack of practical and emotional support.

My partner was not that supportive right after the loss and we had our difficulties; he is better now. I think he is also going through his own struggles and finds it difficult to share. My mum has always been a great support, particularly when I had my miscarriage. My friends have been in touch, but I feel that they do not really understand what I am feeling, and I have been avoiding them as this has just caused me more upset.

6. Other life stressors.

   I think I have suffered from low self-esteem on and off, and this has been a lot worse since my miscarriage. I have been struggling with endometriosis and it was very difficult to conceive.

7. Previous losses.

   My grandmother's death when I was 11. Being diagnosed with endometriosis, and eventually infertility, at around age 30.

CREATING YOUR TIMELINE

Now that you have collected some of the relevant details that help you understand your loss better, let's create a timeline of your loss. Seeing things written down chronologically in your timeline will be vital in helping you to see the bigger picture, and will help your mind put things in order. Make sure you include everything that is relevant – there are probably so many memories and emotions attached to your loss that it is easy to forget some at times, and you might only be focusing on the same selected few, which can leave you feeling stuck. Writing down *all* memories will help you to see your loss in a more balanced way, and help you to feel you are working toward a place where you can feel okay about your loss.

Start with a timeline of all the positive and negative memories around your loss; I want you to list all the upsetting and good memories you have in relation to your loss, including before and since your loss. You can use any format you wish, but what follows is an example that you can use as a template. In the example, you are asked to rate the distress level any negative memory triggers in you when you think about it now, with 0 being no distress at all and 10 being the most you can imagine. All positive memories are to be marked with a "P".

The example below was again completed by Sophia, who had a late miscarriage and had suffered from infertility previously. Please bear in mind that the example below only shows an excerpt of a complete timeline. Your timeline is likely to have at least 15 entries, and there is no limit to how many entries you can include.

TIMELINE OF A LOSS		
AGE/YEAR/ MONTH	**EVENT**	**0-10 OR P**
Age 6 (?)	Playing with my dolls in my bedroom. I loved to play "mummy", and would spend hours dressing, feeding and pushing them around in my little pram. I always wanted to have a younger sibling, but this never happened.	P
Age 28/2015	I meet Matthew and we soon start talking about having a family. We both have a strong wish to have children, and I feel so happy to have finally found someone who I feel I want to spend my life with and who loves children just as much as I do.	P
2017–2018	Struggling to fall pregnant and finally finding out that I have endometriosis, and that this is likely the cause of my infertility. I am shattered – all I ever wanted was to become a mum, and maybe I will never be one now.	7

AGE/YEAR/ MONTH	EVENT	0-10 OR P
June 2019	I find out I am pregnant! We are so happy, but a little anxious at the same time. I tell my mum and she cries with joy.	P
August 2019	We have our 12-week scan. Everything is fine and our baby is healthy. I can finally relax. Matthew and I feel very close.	P
Loss/Miscarriage		
9 October 2019	Finding out during my 19-week ultrasound scan that our baby Lisa has died. Going home and waiting for labour to start. Lots of crying and not leaving the house for days. Feels like my life is ending.	10
12 October 2019	Going back into hospital to be induced. Having to give birth to my baby. They give me lots of medication – everything is a haze. I finally hold Lisa and she is perfect.	9, but also P when I remember holding her
November 2019	Matthew tells me that I need to stop hiding away from everyone and start to think of other things apart from the miscarriage. I feel deeply hurt and we later have a fight; I say to him that he does not need to be with me if I am too much for him. We later make up and apologize, but it is still very painful.	8
December 2019	Christmas and the time leading up to Christmas. I want to hide and not see anyone, but feel I am expected to make an effort. Wherever I am or whoever is with me, all I can think of is my baby girl. The worst Christmas ever. Spending most of my time just with Matthew, at home.	7

AGE/YEAR/ MONTH	EVENT	0-10 OR P
February 2020	Matthew takes me for a special weekend away for Valentine's Day. We have a ceremony for Lisa and have lots of time to talk. We are both still struggling with losing her, but the weekend also reminds me how special Matthew is to me and how beautiful it will be when we will have our little family.	P
March 2020	We decide we want to start trying for a baby again. When I get my period, I end up feeling overcome with pain, and then feel very depressed for a couple of days.	6

YOUR STORY

Creating your story about your loss will help you to make sense of what has happened to you. It will help you to feel understood and more in control of what you are going through. It will also give you some insights into your internal world by linking relevant experiences together and providing a narrative for your emotional difficulties. The purpose of telling your story is not only to express your own experiences and emotions, but also to be heard. So keep in mind that you might want to share your story with others when you feel ready.

Thinking about telling your story about your loss might feel daunting, but rest assured that it is likely to be much easier than you expect. Most of the groundwork has already been laid by you completing the last two exercises in this chapter. You have already collected the important details that need to go into your story – the factors that affect the impact of your loss, and your timeline of important memories. All that is needed now is to write your story from these details and fine-tune it, adding any relevant information that will make your story more meaningful.

THE STRUCTURE (OF A GOOD STORY)

A good story has certain elements to it that are useful to keep in mind; it has structure: a beginning, middle and end. The beginning gives you the background and introduces the main characters. The middle consists of a conflict or struggle the character/s have to go through, and the story ends with a resolution of those struggles.

In your case, your **beginning** will be the memories from before your loss that are relevant to help you and others to fully understand the meaning of your loss. Omitting the beginning of your story will create a lot of confusion, as it provides vital context to how you are feeling now. Start with your first memory related to your loss, and work your way through all the positive and negative memories, until you get to just days or weeks prior to your loss. Include how old you were or in which year/month the events happened.

The **middle** of your story will be about your loss. Here, you should go into great detail about any relevant detail from just before you experienced your loss, the actual loss and the first few days or weeks after your loss happened. Any memory that creates a strong emotional reaction is probably relevant and will need to be included. Including a lot of detail will help your mind to anchor the strong emotions that these distressing memories trigger, and will help you to stay grounded. While acknowledging and accepting all of those feelings, make sure to also include memories and details that made this difficult experience easier or more meaningful. Include who else was there, and the images that have stuck with you, and the worst part of the loss.

Regarding the **end** of your story, you are unlikely just yet to know exactly how your resolution will look; leaving it open-ended is absolutely fine. However, there might be some clues in the details of your story and what has happened since your loss that will give a glimpse of what your ending might look like. Taking into account the positive belief you would like to hold about yourself, you can allow yourself to be creative and imagine what you would like your ending to be. Make sure you write a balanced and realistic account of your positive and negative memories. Include details about the support you have been offered/have received since your loss.

You can write your story in your journal or you can create a typed document. The latter might be easier as you will be making changes to your story in stages.

Once you have completed the first draft of your story, you should congratulate yourself on your achievement. Next, re-read it and pay attention to the following three aspects: characters, emotions and compassion. Make any changes as needed, keeping in mind that the purpose of writing your story is increasing your understanding, helping you process what has happened, and creating a balanced and realistic memory.

1. **Characters:** Make sure all characters relevant to your story are included. What happens to whom and who is causing what? Who has been important to you in your story and why?
2. **Emotions:** Re-read your story and make sure you have described all the important feelings you had about the different events and your loss at the time, as well as since. Make sure you describe how you felt back then rather than how you are feeling about it now; also include how you feel differently now, to make sense of your current situation and what you envisage the future might look like.
3. **Compassion:** After you have completed the above, take a break before returning to your story again.

On returning to your story, think about how you would tell it if it had happened to someone else. Imagine that you have a lot of compassion and understanding for that person. The reason for this is to help you gain a different perspective of your story. Most importantly, thinking of someone else going through what you have been through will help you to detach yourself from your negative feelings about yourself and see the story for what it is. You might find that you are a lot kinder to and more supportive of yourself, and might even see things more clearly. You might notice aspects about yourself you had taken for granted. This practice will make it easier for you to incorporate more balance and compassion in your story.

Make sure to include sentences expressing compassion and understanding for the imagined other person, such as: "She was so upset and in shock about what happened, and she had tried so hard but there was so much going on...", "He tried so hard/has done so well...", "What they really needed was...". After you have told your story from the perspective of a compassionate observer, go back to your own story and turn it back into the first person. You should now be able to see certain events or situations more clearly, or you might notice that the way you were initially telling your story was in some parts one-sided or judgemental. Telling your story from a place of compassion and understanding will make your story feel more complete and will give it a more positive and supportive tone.

The above guidelines on how to write your personal story are there to help you gain the most meaning, understanding and insight regarding your loss. However, if it feels too overwhelming to follow all of the steps above, do what feels right and possible for you at this moment. Your story can be as short or as long as you wish.

PREVIOUS EXPERIENCES OF GRIEF

How you experience events in your life and how you make sense of them is greatly influenced by societal influences and by what you have learnt from those closest to you while growing up. When it comes to losses, you will have experienced a variety throughout your life – some big, some small. You have thus learnt what it means to lose something or someone, which feelings are to be expected and how to cope with your loss. From a young age, your caregivers will have done their best to help you cope with a loss; they may have taught you invaluable skills to deal with your current situation, or their own complex history might have made it more difficult for them to support you in learning how to grieve. In addition, our society and what is happening culturally and historically, influences our attitudes toward loss and grief. To think about how and what you learnt about how to cope with loss is to understand your existence and experience in context. This, in turn, will help you to have compassion for yourself and help you to identify the areas you need to work on.

Every loss we experience will remind us of previous unhealed losses. Any past losses that still feel difficult to remember and come to terms with might affect your current grieving. The reason for this is that if your brain is still trying to find a resolution for your past loss it is likely to find it difficult to find a resolution for your current loss as it does not have a valid "blueprint" of how this difficult situation can be processed and made sense of. If this is the case for you, do not worry – it is really very common.

As we looked at previous losses linked to your current loss in chapter 4, you will probably already have held these in mind when working through the exercises in the previous chapters. However, sometimes it is not until later, or until we write down our timeline, that we notice previous losses and how they have affected us. Make sure to keep your previous losses in mind going forward, and give them enough time. You can always do the exercises in this book solely focusing on your previous losses if you notice that they are still causing you a lot of distress.

The following exercise will focus on exploring your experience of early losses – both in terms of the useful skills you may have learnt, as well as helping you to gain insight into what might still be difficult for you about grieving today.

EXERCISE
How You Learnt to Cope with a Loss as a Child

1. Think about a loss you experienced as a child – maybe you lost your favourite stuffed animal, or a close friend of yours moved away.

2. How did you learn how to handle this loss? Was there anyone there to comfort you or to explain what was happening? Were you allowed to be upset or were you encouraged not to cry, and to move on quickly? How did you decide to cope with loss in the future? What did you decide about yourself/others and life as a result of your experience?

3. Take a moment to reflect on your answers, and whether what you learnt about how to cope with loss back then is how you cope with loss now. Are the feelings you find difficult or easy now the same as back then? Does your early experience of loss give you a clue about why some feelings are easier or more difficult for you?

4. Write down what insight you have gained from this exercise.

We all learn continuously throughout life, and each loss you experience gives you an opportunity to gain new skills and become more confident in coping with loss. It is important to acknowledge all the times you have managed to cope well with a loss, or to cope at all, even if it was difficult! Remembering how you have managed to get through difficult times will remind you of your strengths and help you to gain perspective. In the midst of high emotions and feeling vulnerable, we can forget what it feels like when we do cope.

EXERCISE
Qualities, Coping Strategies and Insights from Previous Losses

1. Think about previous losses you have experienced that no longer feel too distressing to you. For example, the end of a relationship or friendship, leaving school/home to go to university, losing a grandparent or relative, not being successful in a job interview, the end of a time that was important to you (a long trip/holiday, a certain time in your life you really enjoyed), learning of a long-term health condition.

2. How did you manage to deal with your losses? What was helpful and what qualities do you think you gained from coping with each loss?

3. Highlight the qualities, strengths and coping strategies you possess that give you the greatest sense of achievement, or self-control, or resilience, or which make you feel good about yourself in any other way.

REVIEWING YOUR GOALS AND BELIEFS ABOUT YOURSELF

Well done on completing this chapter. Thinking about your own history and experiences is not always easy, and can be exhausting. However, I hope that you have been able to get through the exercises, and experienced the benefits of better understanding your loss and the details of your story. Perhaps your loss is even starting to feel a little less overwhelming, and you are starting to discover some meaning in your experience.

I hope you have noticed how rich your life experiences already are, and how many great skills and qualities you already have or are in the process of acquiring. In the midst of pain and hopelessness, it is essential to take stock of not only what you have lost, but to remember what it is you have gained through being able to cope with your previous losses. This does, of course, not make up for the losses you have had to suffer, but it will help you to see things in a more realistic light.

Take a short moment to think about the story you have written about your loss and yourself. Has it changed how you see your loss and how you see yourself? What is it you have learnt from your loss so far that you would like to take with you going forward?

Now update the ratings of your goals and the beliefs about yourself in relation to your loss, which you identified. Compare them with the ratings in the previous chapters. Again, there is no pressure to improve in huge steps, and sometimes some ratings will get worse before they get better again. If your ratings have improved, even if it is by one point, acknowledge how well you are doing and remember that you will achieve your goals!

TRACKING YOUR GOALS AND PROGRESS

Date:

Rate on a scale of 1–10 to what extent you feel you have already reached these goals, where 1 means not at all and 10 means completely:

My first goal is: _____
Rating: /10
My second goal is: _____
Rating: /10
My third goal is: _____
Rating: /10

Negative belief: _____
Right now, how disturbing does it feel to think of the worst part/moment of your loss and the negative belief about yourself? Rate on a scale of 0–10, where 0 means no disturbance at all and 10 means the most disturbance you can imagine.
Rating: /10

Positive belief: _____
How true does the positive statement feel to you right now when you think about your loss? Rate on a scale of 1–10, where 1 means not true at all and 10 means completely true.
Rating: /10

CHAPTER SUMMARY

- Understanding your loss is a way of making sense of all the chaos and creating order in your own mind. Once you understand and acknowledge the meaning of your loss, it will be easier for you to come to terms with it and cope with your emotions.

- There are certain factors that influence the impact your loss has on you and that might make it more difficult for you to grieve. Being aware of your personal factors helps you to make sense of your emotions and put things into perspective.

- Your timeline will be vital in helping you to see the bigger picture and help your mind to put things in order. Make sure you include everything that is relevant to be able to see your experience in a balanced way.

- Your personal story about your loss will help you to feel understood and more in control of what you are going through. It will also provide you with insights by linking relevant experiences together and providing a narrative for your emotional difficulties.

- Remember all the qualities, insights and coping strategies you have learnt from your previous losses, and that they can help you with grieving your current loss.

7

HELPING YOU TO COPE WITH YOUR EMOTIONS

In this chapter, we will look at how to cope with your emotions. The previous chapters have already provided you with the tools to manage your emotions by accepting and understanding them better. This will have given you the best foundation to help you through your grieving process. Our emotions are skilful in telling us what we need to physically feel and do, and all we need to do is follow them. However, sometimes people find it difficult to know exactly what to do with their emotions. It can also become confusing when we have emotions about emotions! We can experience strong emotions in response to current triggers, but the emotion that is triggered may actually belong to a past experience or trauma, and responding to the current trigger will not help us to resolve the emotion in the long term. There are also situations when we know what we would like or need to do in response to an emotion, but we are unable to do it.

We will also look at:

- The functions of emotions, in order to really understand the purpose of each emotion and how they are useful for our wellbeing and survival.
- The coping mechanisms that are less helpful, as they cause more suffering in the long term.

- The importance of expressing the different emotions we are experiencing in relation to our grief, and how to manage overwhelming emotions when we feel "stuck".
- Each of the main emotions we experience when grieving, and ways to cope with them.

The chapter will conclude with several exercises to help you put what you have learnt into practice.

THE FUNCTIONS OF EMOTIONS

Emotions are complex experiences we all struggle with at times. While there is a need for us to not let emotions run our entire life, and for us to learn appropriate responses to our emotions, we often forget how useful emotions are to us in everyday life. Emotions guide us to overcome obstacles, develop necessary social relationships, and enable us to make accurate and often vital split-second decisions that help our survival and social wellbeing. Take a moment to notice how you feel about emotions – do you have a love/hate relationship with them, do you generally find them bothersome or do you generally feel comfortable with your emotions? Maybe there are some emotions you like and feel confident coping with, while there are others that you find rather challenging?

DIFFERENT EMOTIONS AND THEIR FUNCTIONS		
EMOTION	FUNCTION	EXAMPLE
Anxiety (Panic)	Signalling threat or danger in relation to physical and relational safety (to yourself and others).	Feeling anxious about running into the middle of a busy road. Feeling anxious about a partner's reaction after having lied to them.

EMOTION	FUNCTION	EXAMPLE
Anger (**Frustration**)	Signalling threat or danger in relation to personal boundaries and self-worth (to yourself and others).	Feeling angry about your mother secretly reading your messages on your phone. Feeling angry when you were made redundant while pregnant.
Sadness	Signalling loss and the need to hold on to people/things for survival.	Feeling sad about the end of a romantic relationship. Feeling sad about your father's death.
Depression (**Feeling hopeless/ empty or persistently worthless/ having no motivation or interest in anything**)	Signalling needing to turn away from life and retreat inwards, focusing all energy on what needs to be addressed internally while avoiding any further possible negative external experiences. Signalling needing to cope with a loss, and/or with being subordinate and/or defeated and/or trapped. *Warning: depression only serves a function when mild and temporary and in extreme situations. Severe and longstanding depression can indicate a mental health problem.*	Feeling depressed for a period of time after finding out you have terminal cancer. Feeling depressed about being trapped in a job where you are bullied by your managers, but you cannot afford to resign. *Clinical depression (mental health problem): experiencing symptoms of medium to severe depression for six months or longer after your partner has broken up with you. See chapter 9.*
Guilt	Signalling violation of moral code and the threat of possible consequences.	Feeling guilty about knowingly not having paid for an item when going through a supermarket self-checkout. Feeling guilty about not having been supportive toward your friend when he was going through a rough time.

EMOTION	FUNCTION	EXAMPLE
Shame	Signalling violation of important social rules and norms and the threat of rejection and exclusion from social groups. Guiding our (social) behaviours for the benefit of society. *Warning: A lot of the shame we experience is not functional and often belongs to a past traumatic experience.*	Feeling ashamed about parking in a disabled space when not eligible. Feeling ashamed about not having taken a shower or washed your hands in a week. *Non-functional shame: Feeling ashamed for not being asked on a date by a potential mate. Feeling ashamed for not being able to afford an expensive holiday with friends.*
Excitement	Signalling reward and pleasure.	Feeling excited about going on holiday.
Contentment	Signalling safety and wellbeing, confirming our self-worth.	Feeling content about having moved to the countryside and having more time for yourself and your family.
Love and Affection	Signalling safety, protection and belonging, confirming self-worth and valuing others.	Feeling love for your children.

Can you imagine what life would be like without these emotions? You would be prone to being physically and emotionally hurt all the time if you did not feel any anxiety; you would even be much more likely to die or get seriously injured, as there would be no signal to not do something dangerous. Your relationships would likely be unstable or short-lived if you had no anxiety about doing something that could upset or hurt another person. If you never felt any anger, you would likely end up getting used and exploited, and end up having little self-worth and self-belief. Without anger you would not know when to protect yourself and your loved ones. If you never felt sadness, you would probably easily leave relationships behind and put little effort into keeping strong connections, leaving you vulnerable when you might need help or support. Without guilt or shame you would not be careful about living in line with your values and goals, which would put your own wellbeing and the wellbeing of others at risk.

HOW *NOT* TO COPE WITH YOUR EMOTIONS

Your brain is programmed to deal with your loss and process what has happened to you, so that you can move on from it. However, it can only do its job if you let it! So, when you feel different emotions and thoughts about your loss and when memories emerge, it's important to give yourself the space and time to let these emotions be, to remember what has happened, and allow your mind to find resolutions. Sometimes, your emotions will also mean that you have to take action or learn from your experiences, so you can avoid similar situations in the future.

Actively avoiding your emotions, thoughts and memories will slow down your grieving process and prolong the pain. Remember that some avoidance (which is not harmful, as outlined in a moment) is absolutely normal, and can help you take a break from your grieving. However, avoidance becomes problematic when it becomes a habit and dominates your way of coping.

Avoidance can be passive, which means not doing something to avoid triggering emotions and memories, such as withdrawing from life and isolating yourself. Avoidance can also be active, such as throwing yourself into activities (sport, alcohol, sex, etc.) to distract yourself from emotions and memories. The importance of finding out whether you are engaging in avoidance behaviour is not only because the activity could be harmful to you, but to be able to understand the intention behind it.

For example, if you feel like staying in by yourself and not seeing others for a while, it could be that you need some time to reflect on things, to take care of yourself and to have the time and space to process your loss. This would not be avoidance behaviour. However, if you were to stay in with the intention of not seeing others as you know it will remind you of your loss and upset you, then you are probably avoiding emotions.

The same is true with sex, intimacy and dating. It can be very nourishing and healing and will help you to feel connected to yourself, others and life again. However, if it is done compulsively and without truly connecting to others, it is unlikely to make you feel better in the long term, and you may be using it to avoid feelings you find too difficult to face.

When it comes to alcohol and drugs, many people find it easy to use them to get away from difficult feelings, even if only temporarily – "having a drink" is so engrained in our culture. Before you drink or take any drugs, remember the saying, "Drinking today is borrowing happiness from tomorrow!". Nobody would deny that drinking alcohol or taking drugs can make you feel better in the moment, but after you stop and the pleasurable effects wear off, depression and other uncomfortable feelings and physical symptoms set in. If you are struggling already with low mood and chaotic emotions, the aftermath of drinking or drug-taking could be truly awful. You already have a lot on your plate; don't make things even harder for yourself.

Please be particularly careful about using any addictive behaviour or substances to avoid your emotions and memories.

HOW TO COPE WITH YOUR EMOTIONS

How to cope with your emotions better includes accepting your emotions, expressing your emotions, using "affect regulation tools" and challenging your thoughts and beliefs. Each approach is helpful, and a combination of all four approaches is guaranteed to help you become more confident in dealing with your emotions, and to feel calmer and more in control in the long term.

ACCEPTING YOUR EMOTIONS

Accepting your emotions is an important tool when it comes to grieving. There are times when it is important to act when we feel an emotion, as this will alleviate what we are feeling – but sometimes just being with and *accepting* the emotion will be the most effective coping strategy you can use. In grief, we are unable to do anything that could greatly alleviate our suffering, as we simply have to feel sad and feel the loss until it runs its course. Apart from sadness, there are other emotions in relation to losing someone or something that we are often unable to do anything about. Maybe you feel regret or anger about something that happened in the past in relation to your loss. Often, you cannot go back and change this, so acceptance and allowing yourself to just feel and express all emotions is the most useful action you can do to help yourself. Remember, emotions are not permanent, and they will always pass if you accept them rather than fighting them. If you feel you need to improve your skills in accepting emotions, go back to chapter 4 and remind yourself of the key points and techniques.

EXPRESSING YOUR GRIEF

Expressing your grief will give you instant relief and will help you move forward. Expressing your grief and emotions can take many shapes and forms: crying, talking to others, journaling, letter writing, exercising, being creative, or engaging in rituals. There is no right way to express grief and emotion; the key is to for you to find a way that will help you personally. By expressing your emotions, you will be able to release them. You might have to express your grief numerous times, but eventually you will feel lighter, and be able to move through your grief rather than being stuck. Use the grieving time you have set aside for yourself (as discussed in chapter 3) to express your grief and emotions.

Crying is one of the most common ways to express your sadness, but also other emotions, in relation to your grief – feeling angry, desperate, anxious, overwhelmed, etc.). Many people find crying a natural and effective way to express their emotions, and one that brings instant relief.

Talking to others and communicating your loss and all the emotions it brings you is a great way to express your grief. You can talk to others about anything that is on your mind or you feel stuck with, whether this is present or past. If you really want to benefit from talking to someone and resolve your loss, tell your story. Sharing your story with different people and getting different reactions, and indeed just telling your story over and over again, will help you to process your grief. Telling your story will not only help to release your emotions, but – even more importantly – will allow you to feel heard and understood and for your emotions to be acknowledged.

When you tell your story to others, you will find some reactions more helpful than others. Don't worry if telling your story does not always go well, and be patient with those listening to you. The most helpful listeners are those who are able to just take in what you have to say, acknowledge it, and reflect back what they are hearing without trying to make things better or pointing out the silver lining. The key is to have several people you tell your story to, and you will most certainly benefit from it greatly.

EXERCISE
Telling Your Story

1. Chose a person you would like to tell your story to and arrange to meet them somewhere where you feel safe and able to talk in private. You can mention to them that you would really appreciate it if you could talk to them about what has happened to you.

2. Before you meet them, read through your story again and the key points you want to get across. Don't worry about forgetting any parts or telling it exactly the way you have written it. Trust yourself that, however you tell your story, it will be exactly the right way for this particular moment in time and this person.

3. Before you tell your story, make a note of any fears or worries you have – if any. Perhaps you are worried that the other person will blame you for the loss, or that they won't be interested in hearing your story. Be understanding toward yourself, and acknowledge that these fears are normal.

4. After you have told your story, reflect and make a note of anything you have learnt from this experience. How do you feel, having told someone your story? Did you feel understood? Did you feel your emotions were acknowledged? If so, how did this affect how you feel about your loss? Was anything the other person said or how they reacted helpful, and did they make you see what happened to you in a slightly different light? Do you feel they liked listening to your story and appreciated you sharing it with them? (If in doubt, you can always ask them directly!) Who else might be a good person to tell your story to?

FINDING YOUR WAY THROUGH LOSS & GRIEF

Journaling and **letter writing** can be immensely helpful in your grieving process, not only to help you express your grief, but to help you make sense, find new meaning, distance yourself form the intensity of your emotions and to help you process what has happened. Go back to chapter 3 to remind yourself of why writing down your thoughts and feelings is so important and effective. You might also want to revisit the exercise on writing a letter to your loss in chapter 5.

Exercising, or using your body, is also a great way to express and release your emotions. Next time you feel a strong emotion, notice where you feel this in your body. You will likely feel some tension, a charge or other discomfort that will naturally make you want to do something; but we often feel restrained or at a loss as to what to do with all this extra uncomfortable energy. From a physiological viewpoint, doing something active will actually change your body's biochemistry in terms of hormones such as cortisol, serotonin and adrenalin. What is important is that you choose an activity that is right for you personally and right for the emotion. For example, forcing yourself to be calm and practise yoga when you are feeling angry might make you angrier (but yoga might be a great activity to do when you're anxious).

In general, anger will be released when you do something active that releases a lot of energy, such as hitting a punch bag or going for a run while listening to fast and loud music. Anxiety is helped by any activity that will make you feel more grounded and also uses up energy, as your body will need to get rid of all the energy and hormones that get you ready for "fight or flight".

Going for a walk, especially in pleasant surroundings, is something that most people find helpful, whatever their mood. The rhythm of walking, together with moving through different surroundings, can help you get unstuck in your thoughts and help you get a different viewpoint.

Other ways of using your body to help with emotions include hugging someone when upset to feel more connected, cleaning when angry or anxious or to regain a sense of control, or being silly with your friends or children. Be creative and try out different things until you find what works for you. Don't overthink it, just do it!

Being creative, such as through art and music, can help to release and process your emotions, reduce stress and anxiety, increase self-esteem and support self-discovery. Sing the songs you feel most drawn to, or listen to them while driving in the car, or dance along when no one is watching! Playing an instrument, painting, cooking, knitting, etc. are also great.

Rituals can carry great meaning; they can release emotions and help you feel more connected, give you more purpose, and bring peace. Rituals have been part of human existence for thousands of years, whether cultural, spiritual or religious. Especially in relation to loss, rituals seem helpful in marking this important transition and easing us through it. You might find solace in taking part in established rituals, or you might want to create your own.

What you would like to achieve through your ritual can be anything: commemorating what you have lost, symbolizing letting go of what has been lost, bringing peace and clarity into your life, clearing your mind and body of difficult feelings, strengthening a positive connection, or making a clear break with someone or something that has been negative in your life. Some examples of what people do as their "ritual" are: lighting a candle or incense while making a wish, saying affirmations or prayers, going to a place in nature that has great meaning to them or brings great comfort, carrying with them or holding an item that makes them feel positive and might be connected to their loss, writing a letter or a note and burning or burying it, or throwing away things that are connected to something negative or the loss.

AFFECT REGULATION TOOLS

When your emotions feel particularly difficult, intense and overwhelming, and none of the other techniques, including acceptance, seem possible or they are not working, using "affect regulation tools" can be a quick and easy way to help you feel more balanced again and reduce any discomfort and distress.

Mindfulness, meditation and breathing techniques are great tools for regulating emotions. There are many free sources and courses available online that can help you learn and practise them.

Another way to help you regulate your emotions easily and quickly is the Spiral Technique.[12]

EXERCISE
Spiral Technique

1. Notice the disturbing feelings and/or memory, and concentrate on where you sense these emotions in your body (chest, belly, throat, arms, head, etc.).
2. Imagine that the feelings are "energy". If it is a spiral of energy, which direction is it moving in: clockwise or counter-clockwise? (There is no right or wrong answer, just go with what comes up first).
3. Focus on the feelings and change the direction of the spiral to the opposite direction. Notice what happens to your feelings and sensations as you keep the spiral going (in the opposite direction). Many people find that their emotions and sensations disappear or lessen.
4. If the feelings begin to disappear, then continue until you feel comfortable.

CHALLENGING YOUR THOUGHTS AND BELIEFS

Our emotions are tightly linked with our thoughts. The way we feel influences our thoughts, and vice versa. You can take advantage of the thoughts, that underpin your emotions by noticing them and challenging them in order to help you feel differently or to decrease the emotional intensity. Challenging your thoughts is an effective and well-researched Cognitive Behavioural Therapy (CBT) technique.

How Thoughts and Beliefs Influence Our Emotions and Behaviours

To illustrate how thoughts influence emotions, let's look at three different thought responses to being made redundant at work, and compare how interpreting the same situation in different ways has a direct effect on our emotions and behaviours.

Here is an example of how thoughts and beliefs about losing your job influence your behaviours and emotions.

THOUGHTS/ BELIEFS	CONSEQUENCES/ BEHAVIOURS	CONSEQUENCES/ EMOTIONS
Person A "It's my fault and I should have worked harder. I am probably just incompetent and never deserved the job in the first place."	Procrastinate about finding a new job and avoid applying for highly skilled jobs due to lack of confidence and fear of failure. Ruminate about what went wrong.	Low and helpless. Anxious about the prospect of finding/ losing another job in the future.

THOUGHTS/ BELIEFS	CONSEQUENCES/ BEHAVIOURS	CONSEQUENCES/ EMOTIONS
Person B "I know that my boss and most of my colleagues never liked me, and it is obvious that I was targeted and made redundant. There are lots of my colleagues who do not work as hard as I do, so it's really unfair I was made to go."	Ruminate about how unfairly you have been treated. Approach new jobs and interviews in a defensive and guarded manner.	Anger/resentment. Anxiety/mistrust toward future employers and colleagues.
Person C "I know that the company was struggling for a long time and needed to cut jobs; strategically, my position was an easy target. There might have been things I would have done differently, but on the whole I received great feedback from my boss. I know I deserve a good job."	Accept and move on from your loss after a brief period of grieving your old job. Apply for new jobs and plan for new opportunities in the future. Network with possible employers.	Some understandable sadness, disappointment and anger, but not intense or long-lasting. Calm, positive and confident about finding another job.

You will probably agree that Person C is going to cope much better than Persons A or B. Person C has a realistic view of the situation, which makes them feel less anxious, sad and angry and helps them to move on from their loss by taking the right actions.

Automatic Thoughts and Feelings

It's very common for people to hold beliefs similar to those seen in Persons A and B, as most of us tend to hold negative beliefs about ourselves and others when in a stressful situation – it's an automatic response. We will usually jump to a conclusion in a matter of seconds when something happens to us. These instant thoughts are called "automatic thoughts"; they often raise strong feelings in ourselves that might feel overwhelming.

You might not always be conscious of your automatic thoughts, and they can be difficult to notice unless you actively try to identify them. In fact, what you will often notice first are the *emotions* triggered by your thoughts. Having automatic thoughts does not always mean that you are actually thinking in sentences. Instead, you might have flashes of images – either imagined or memories – which will describe the thought you have. Identifying your automatic thought is therefore often more like decoding what is going through your mind as a mixture of images and words and giving it a distinct description that is more tangible.

A way to train yourself to become more aware of your automatic thoughts is to notice when you feel strong emotions and to ask yourself what was going through your mind at that moment. Identify any images, or what you were saying to yourself. Sometimes our initial thoughts are quite vague, and we have to dig deeper to get to their real meaning and the beliefs we hold about ourselves and others. Let's say that you lose your job and you are feeling anxious and panicky. The initial automatic thought you might identify is, "It should not have happened." This thought does not really tell you a lot about what you think/believe about yourself or others, nor does it explain your anxiety and panic. So, challenging this belief is unlikely to shift your emotions greatly. To get to the meaning behind this thought, you can ask yourself:

"What's the worst thing about losing my job?"

"The worst thing is that I worked so hard and gave everything in this job and I still lost my job."

"And what's the worst thing about that?"

"The worst thing about that is that if I lost my job even though I worked hard, it must mean that I am incompetent and will never be able to hold a good job."

The key thought and belief about yourself and the meaning behind the initial thought of "It should not have happened" is, therefore, "I am incompetent and will never be able to hold a good job."

Anyone holding this belief is likely going to feel very hopeless and anxious. It probably also feels like a very convincing statement/belief, given that you have just lost your job.

It is important to remind ourselves that automatic thoughts and feelings can be very "hit and miss". We are constantly experiencing and learning new things every day, so there is a huge pool of complex information stored in our brain that will create these automatic thoughts in a split-second. Initial reactions can, of course, be spot on, and the judgements we make are drawn from what we have learnt and experienced over our whole lifetime; however, sometimes what we have learnt about ourselves in the past is no longer valid, or our conclusion is drawn from limited experiences and sources of information.

Challenging Your Thoughts and Beliefs

Regardless of what your beliefs are and how many negative automatic thoughts you have about a situation, you can learn to step back and reflect and challenge unhelpful beliefs and thoughts.

I want to stress that we are not trying to convince you to believe something that does not feel authentic or is far from the truth. Instead, we want you to learn to see situations in a more realistic way and to open up to seeing things and yourself from different perspectives. The difficulty with our initial reaction to situations and our automatic thoughts is that they are "automatic", and do not necessarily reflect our whole knowledge or insight. Our initial reaction to a difficult situation also often triggers past losses or difficult experiences, and our reactions can be strongly influenced by what we have still not come to terms with in the past; and when past difficult experiences are triggered, our ability to see things in a balanced way is almost impossible. We need to make an effort to differentiate between how realistic our thoughts and beliefs are, and what belongs to a trauma and experience we have had in the past.

You need to step back and look at your thoughts and beliefs, and update the ones that are no longer of use to you and are probably outdated. We all learn throughout life and become wiser, and challenging your automatic thoughts and your usual reaction to a loss is an opportunity to learn seeing things – and yourself – differently. Perhaps you have already gained some insight by reading this book.

To help you look at a situation differently and challenge your thoughts, imagine what you would say to a friend who was going through the same situation. Would you come to the same conclusions? What other aspects would you take into account, and would you be seeing things in a more balanced way?

Another way to see what is really going on is to imagine you are in court and you have to defend your thoughts and beliefs in front of a wise and fair judge. Cross-examine yourself, and question every aspect of what has happened and how you are making sense of it. If you believe you have lost your job because you are a failure, what is the evidence for this thought that you would present in court? Is there any evidence that you have failed more than is normally expected by an employee? Are there any management reviews to back this up? What about successes – were there none? Have you failed in previous jobs? How can you be so sure of what you believe to be the reason you lost your job? Are there any other factors that might have played a part in the company making you redundant? ... and so on.

Challenging your thoughts will help reduce the intensity of your difficult feelings and distress. We are not looking at changing your difficult feelings completely into positive ones (which would be an unrealistic expectation), but any reduction will help you to feel less triggered by the situation and will help you to change your beliefs about yourself. Once your intense feelings about a situation or memory have changed, you are less likely to think about it as frequently and you will be able to move on from it.

EXERCISE
Challenging Your Thoughts

1. Write down a trigger, which can be a situation or a memory that you are struggling with and is causing you distress or discomfort.
2. Identify your feelings and rate their intensity, with 10 being the highest intensity.
3. Write down the automatic thoughts and beliefs that come to your mind when thinking about your trigger. Remember that you might have to ask yourself "What's the worst thing about that?" to get to the underlying key belief.
4. Challenge your thoughts and beliefs by looking at the evidence and alternative ways of looking at the situation (for example, applying the situation to a friend, or self-cross-examination).
5. Write down alternative, more realistic thoughts and beliefs, taking into account the insights you have gained from challenging your thoughts in step 4.

6. Identify how you feel about your trigger now. Write down all the feelings you initially identified and re-rate their intensity. Add any new feelings and rate those as well.

CHALLENGING YOUR THOUGHTS				
Trigger – situation or memory	Automatic thoughts and beliefs	Feelings Intensity (0–10)	Alternative, more realistic thoughts and beliefs	Feelings change Intensity (0–10)
Meeting with friends at the weekend and finding out that my ex-colleague was promoted.	Nobody cared about me and my efforts; they could not wait to see me go. I'm not important.	Angry 9/10 Sad 6/10	I know that they were working on restructuring the company, and my redundancy and her promotion might have been part of this. It's not fair and I don't think I deserved this, but I also know that she had more experience than me. My friends from work actually came to see me this weekend, so they must care. I do know that I am important to my friends and to my boyfriend.	Angry 4/10 Sad 3/10

DEALING WITH SPECIFIC EMOTIONS

Below are some insights and specific coping strategies for your emotions.

ANXIETY (PANIC)

Helpful Insights

- Anxiety is rooted in past experiences and what we have learnt from caregivers about when we need to protect ourselves and others. Sometimes this reaction can be helpful (if there is an actual threat), but sometimes our response is unhelpful or exaggerated.
- Any perceived or actual threat will trigger a fight or flight response in you, which will make it difficult to see a situation clearly and in an unbiased way in that very moment.
- Thinking and worrying a lot about a perceived threat is often driven by us believing that it makes us prepared and gives us more control over the situation or problem; paradoxically, it fuels anxiety and hence makes us less prepared and in control.
- Avoidance is a common and understandable response, but unless what you fear is an actual immediate threat to your survival, it usually creates more problems.
- Anxiety feels terrible, but it's not dangerous and often subsides quickly once we have faced the fear.

Coping Strategies

- Practise acceptance.
- Be understanding and supportive toward yourself. You are not doing anything wrong and may have every reason to feel anxious. Try not to criticize yourself for feeling anxious or for what you think feeling anxious says about you (that

you are weak, a failure, etc.). Looking after yourself will help you calm your nervous system and cope better.

- Talk to someone about what is making you anxious; having your feelings acknowledged can often make you feel better instantly.
- Face your fears in small steps. Try not to overthink it and just do it – the anxiety you feel beforehand is often worse than the actual experience, and you will usually feel much better for having done it.
- When you feel fairly calm, challenge your anxious automatic thoughts to gain some perspective.
- To let go of your worries, problem-solve what you feel anxious about and schedule in when you can action those solutions, and then focus on something else. If there is no action you can take to solve your worry, acknowledge that you have no control over it and work on acceptance.
- Learn to accept uncertainty. Allowing the discomfort and anxiety about uncertainty is difficult, but once you are no longer battling with it, it will become more manageable.
- Use relaxation activities or exercises to help you feel less anxious, such as listening to music, meditation, breathing exercises and mindfulness – these will help you to feel less anxious and more ready to face your fears and see things more realistically.
- Seek constructive support and advice, but refrain from seeking constant reassurance from others or the internet.
- Exercise helps lower the levels of stress hormones in your body.

ANGER (FRUSTRATION)

Helpful Insights
- Anger is a normal, healthy and protective response to something unfair or threatening happening to us.

- Some people benefit from learning to be more in touch with their anger if they have been suppressing it for a long time. Others benefit from learning to not use anger as the "go-to emotion" when something difficult happens, rather than engaging with other more vulnerable emotions.
- Some people find anger very frightening, or think that it is selfish or harmful to feel and/or express anger.
- Many people find it hard to know what to do with their anger or how to express it constructively.
- Anger is often a result of a lack of confidence in setting clear and healthy boundaries and "the disease to please" (giving too much, or not saying when you feel uncomfortable about how you are being treated), until it becomes all too much and anger erupts.

Coping Strategies

- Practise acceptance.
- Be understanding and supportive toward yourself. You may have every right to be angry. Calm your anger by acknowledging that it's okay to feel this way.
- Be mindful of how you express your anger. If your anger is too intense to think rationally, take some time out and allow yourself to calm down before taking action. Things you say or do in anger cannot be undone, and can often be harmful to you and others.
- Likewise, if you tend to supress your anger and appease others, take your time to think through your response – you can always bring up the issue at a later time if you did not feel able to respond in the moment.
- Talk to someone you can express your anger to, and have a good moan. Often just saying things out loud and being acknowledged resolves the anger so we can move on or feel empowered to take the right action.

- Learn to avoid passive-aggressive communication and be more assertive – be direct, stay with the facts, don't appease or attack. The formula "Fact – Feel – Want" – stating the facts of the situation that make you angry, how you feel about it and what you want – is a very effective assertiveness tool.
- When you feel fairly calm, challenge your angry automatic thoughts to gain some perspective. Pay attention to what you *imagine* other people's possible intention was for treating you this way. Is there another way to explain what happened?
- To release the feeling of intense anger, imagine what you would like to say or do to the person who made you angry. Anything is allowed – your thoughts are yours alone, and whatever you imagine does not mean that you are a bad person or that you would actually do anything you imagine in real life. Often allowing yourself to express the full intensity of your anger in your imagination makes it diminish quickly.
- Write a letter or email to the person you feel angry with, expressing everything you want to say to them, *without* sending it. Keep writing for as long as you feel angry, until there is no anger left!
- Use exercise, such as running, boxing or anything else vigorous, while thinking of what makes you angry, to release tension. Listening to loud or fast music can also feel empowering and be effective.

SADNESS

Helpful Insights
- Sadness is a normal and healthy response to any loss we experience.

- Many struggle with the feeling that being sad means to be weak, or fear that they will be rejected by others if they express their sadness.
- The more you ignore or suppress your sadness, the bigger and more overwhelming your sadness will become.
- Many fear that if they "give in" to their sadness, it will never stop or it will take over everything in their life.
- Sadness can feel overpowering and exhausting, but it is a feeling that will run its course quicker the less you try to suppress it.

Coping Strategies

- Practise acceptance.
- Be understanding and supportive toward yourself. Try to really understand what you are sad about and why. Acknowledging and giving space to your sadness will help you to release your sadness and move through it quicker.
- Talk to someone about what is making you sad. Telling someone how you feel, and having your feelings acknowledged, can often make you feel better instantly.
- The most effective way to release feelings of sadness is to cry. If you struggle to get in touch with your sadness or to cry, you might find it helpful to watch a sad movie, listen to music that makes you emotional, or read stories of others who have had a similar experience to you.
- Write in your journal about what makes you feel sad.
- If you have not allowed yourself to be sad for a long time, or you are in the immediate aftermath of a significant loss, your sadness might feel overwhelming. If you worry about the intensity, schedule in times when you can allow yourself to give in fully to your sadness, and set a time limit. When the time is over, imagine leaving what you feel sad about in an imaginary safe place (for example a treasure box, a vault), and promise yourself to get back to

it when you have next scheduled in some time. Then carry on with the rest of your day.

DEPRESSION

Helpful Insights

- Depression can be seen as an evolutionary adaptation to dealing with (repeated) setbacks and losses. It signals needing to turn away from life and retreat inward – to "reassess" what is happening, while avoiding further potentially stressful external experiences.
- Feeling depressed for short periods of times is a normal human experience.
- A common feature of depression is the suppression of emotions. This happens automatically and unconsciously and keeps you safe from all the difficult and overwhelming emotions, but also robs you from all the pleasurable emotions that make you feel positive, hopeful and "alive".
- While going through a depressive episode, your thinking and awareness is likely to be clouded, and it might be difficult for you to imagine ever feeling better again, or to remember a time you were not depressed.
- A depressive episode can last from a day to several months (or longer if you are suffering from clinical depression). There are many things you can do to help you move through a depressive episode quicker.
- If you are feeling depressed or persistently low for several months, seek professional help.
- For symptoms of depression, see chapter 9.

Coping Strategies

- Practise acceptance.
- Be understanding and supportive toward yourself. Try to understand what might have brought on your depression.

- Acknowledging and recognizing your difficulties will help you to move on to thinking about what might help you resolve them.
- Be patient with yourself. You are doing your best you can and, as hard as it is, getting out of a depressive episode does take time.
- Make sure you are supported and have someone to talk to about how you feel. Talking and connecting to others is hugely important when you are depressed. Depression can make you undermine yourself and your struggles, and you may blame yourself for "not coping better"; a trusted person might help you see things more realistically.
- Suppressing emotions can keep you depressed. If you are noticing a lack of emotion, interest or motivation, try to find out which feelings you might be suppressing, as engaging with them should help you move through your depression quicker. Is there anything making you feel sad or angry? If so, engage with memories connected to those feelings.
- Having a routine and exercising are great antidepressants. You might find it hard to stick to a routine or to exercise when you are depressed, but most people will feel a significant improvement if they do. Be realistic and set yourself small targets. Engage in activities and behaviours that you usually enjoy and you feel confident in.
- There will be days when you will want to do very little, and that is okay. Sometimes, we truly need a good rest – listen to your body and what it needs. However, be aware that having more than several days like this in a row could be a sign that you are trying to avoid places and experiences that you will have to face at some point to get out of your depression.
- When you feel ready, challenge your depressive thoughts and beliefs to gain some perspective. It might take a little while to shift your feelings, but don't give up, and be patient with yourself.

GUILT

Helpful Insights

- Guilt can often make us feel powerless and stuck – if we violate our own moral code we find it difficult to forgive ourselves.
- Self-reproach will not change what we have done, but taking reparative action and supporting ourselves to act differently in the future will make a positive difference now and in the future.
- Sometimes long-standing guilt can be protection from other feelings one is not comfortable with, such as anger.
- Intense guilt can be a sign of clinical depression.

Coping Strategies

- Practise acceptance.
- Be understanding and supportive toward yourself. Try to define what you are feeling guilty about. Ask yourself what is so important to you about this situation and why you feel so guilty about having responded this way.
- Challenge your guilty thoughts to gain some perspective. Would you judge someone else in the same way as you do yourself?
- Depending on what you feel guilty about, is there anything you would like to do to repair what you have done? It can be anything from an apology to a gesture. If so, do what you need to do and move on. There is no need for repeated apologies or gestures.
- When you feel ready, make a conscious decision to start forgiving yourself for what you have done. Holding on to guilt is unhelpful for all; you are more likely to do good for yourself and others when you are in a healthy and happy mindset.
- If there is something in your life you keep feeling guilty about and struggle to move on from, ask yourself what

harm would be caused by letting go of the guilt. The answer will show you the belief you hold about the "protective" role of guilt, and you are then able to start working on dismantling the belief's validity. For example, "Guilt helps me feel closer to the person I have lost as it keeps me thinking about them." Here, guilt is acting as protection against sadness.

SHAME

Helpful Insights
- Shame is a very powerful feeling as it goes right to the core of our sense of self-worth.
- The most intense and painful shame we feel is often a result of a past traumatic experience. It is a result of someone, or a group, having tried to control our behaviours and feelings by purposefully shaming us. For example, feeling ashamed of your body because when you were growing up your mother would tell you that you were fat.
- Shame usually makes us turn away or hide to protect ourselves.
- Often, facing our shameful feelings and experiences can help us to demystify and take away power from the feeling, as we discover that what we were told was shameful is really not that bad at all.

Coping Strategies
- Practise acceptance.
- Be understanding and supportive toward yourself. The feeling of shame is very powerful, and instantly makes us feel vulnerable and horrible about ourselves. You don't need to try to fight the feeling, but you also don't need to accept it as a fact; that is "Because I feel so much shame,

I must have done something very shameful/I must be very shameful."

- Try to define what you are feeling shameful about. When and how did you learn that this is shameful?
- Battling your shameful thoughts is usually not effective and only makes them stronger. Instead, be curious and listen to what the intention of the shameful feeling is; for example, is it "trying to make you a better person", or "protecting you from being shamed by others", or "making you as likeable as possible, so you don't have to be lonely?" The key is to take on board what the shame is trying to achieve, and then decide whether there might be more helpful ways of achieving this.
- If there are particular incidents that have made you feel ashamed, facing and "dismantling" the experiences can be very helpful. Make sure you feel calm and rested, then take some time remembering what happened. Pause your memory at the moment you experienced the most intense shame, and investigate what was actually happening around you. Rather than looking away (what we usually do when we are ashamed), look at the people around you who made you feel ashamed or who were witnessing your shameful experience. What was going on for them? What facial expression did they have? What were motivating their behaviour? Say whatever you feel you would have wanted to say to them. Pausing the experience will make it easier to face your shame and give you the time to see the bigger picture. Facing those who make you feel ashamed can be very powerful, as it shows that they can no longer control or suppress you.

REVIEWING YOUR GOALS AND BELIEFS ABOUT YOURSELF

This chapter has described many techniques and ideas about how to better cope with your emotions. You might want to take some time to digest it all and to continue trying out different techniques to see what works for you. It's important to keep in mind that, sometimes, we need to try out a new skill several times before it works, and not all skills and techniques work for every situation and problem.

The bottom line is that any time you dedicate to better cope with your emotions is helpful, and you will always learn something new about yourself. We all have a natural tendency to want to heal ourselves and to learn to adapt and cope better with life. The more time we allow ourselves for this process, and the more ideas and solutions we present to our minds, the easier it will be to find the solutions to our problems.

Which skill/s or technique/s have you found most helpful for which emotion, so far? Which skills/techniques would you like to become more confident in? Which emotions are you still struggling with and might need more attention to find the right coping strategies for?

Please update the ratings for your goals and the beliefs about yourself in relation to your loss, which you identified. Compare them with the ratings in the previous chapters. Notice any change. Remember that in the long term, we want your ratings to improve, but it is completely normal for things to get worse before they get better, or to move toward improvement in a non-linear fashion and have times of stagnation.

TRACKING YOUR GOALS AND PROGRESS

Date:

Rate on a scale of 1–10 to what extent you feel you have already reached these goals, where 1 means not at all and 10 means completely:

My first goal is: _____
Rating: /10
My second goal is: _____
Rating: /10
My third goal is: _____
Rating: /10

Negative belief: _____
Right now, how disturbing does it feel to think of the worst part/moment of your loss and the negative belief about yourself? Rate on a scale of 0–10, where 0 means no disturbance at all and 10 means the most disturbance you can imagine.
Rating: /10

Positive belief: _____
How true does the positive statement feel to you right now when you think about your loss? Rate on a scale of 1–10, where 1 means not true at all and 10 means completely true.
Rating: /10

CHAPTER SUMMARY

- Emotions are really useful, as they guide us to overcome obstacles, develop necessary social relationships and enable us to make split-second decisions that help our survival and social wellbeing.

- Habitually avoiding your emotions, thoughts and memories will slow down your grieving process and prolong the pain. Be careful about using any addictive behaviours or substances to avoid your feelings and memories.

- Using one of the four approaches to cope with your emotions – accepting your emotions, expressing your emotions, using affect regulation tools and challenging your thoughts and beliefs – will help you to become more confident in dealing with your emotions and to feel calmer and more in control in the long term.

- There are specific coping strategies for each emotion that can further help you resolve your difficulties and manage your feelings.

- The best way to use the emotion coping strategies in this chapter is to try out different techniques, maybe multiple times, to see what works for you personally.

8

COPING WITH AND ADAPTING TO CHANGE

As we have looked at understanding your grief better and helping you to process what has happened and cope with your emotions, you might feel ready to take further steps to adapt to your new life. Most people will take some time to get to this point in their grieving process. Change can be difficult, as adapting to the changes brought on by your loss can make your loss feel very real – that what has been, is no longer, and that there is no going back. However, most people will arrive at a point in their grieving process where they notice themselves feeling increasingly ready to build their life up again, and are more confident and hopeful about their future.

What I will help you with in this chapter is to cope with the change you are currently going through. We will look at the connection between grieving and change, the process of adapting to change, addressing the difficulties you might be experiencing around change, and finally how to adapt to and embrace your new reality.

THE CONNECTION BETWEEN GRIEVING AND CHANGE

To help you understand the importance of adapting to change, and how closely grief and change are connected, take a step back and have a look at your whole life and what you have been through since you were born. I want you to appreciate all the changes you have been through and all the losses you have had to grieve. Can you notice the multitude of experiences that make up your life, that you have already coped with?

Life is dynamic: we start relationships and lose them, babies are born, children grow up and move away, projects and interests are invested in and forgotten, jobs and careers are started and sometimes end only to move in another direction. In the context of the wider world, exciting possibilities in technologies and how we cope with problems such as illnesses and societal problems arise, but life continues to move on and we try our best to keep up with all the change. Most of the time we do exceptionally well at coping and adapting. However, it is only natural that we sometimes feel overwhelmed, and then struggle to, or resist, adapting to change.

Every loss in our life leads to change, so adapting to change is an essential part of the grieving process. Likewise, every change in our life includes a period of mourning of what is left behind – whether we actively chose to make the change or not.

Grieving the loss and dealing with the emotions of loss is only one part of the process; the next step is to deal with new challenges and prepare for the future. This often requires a period of learning new skills, exploring new opportunities and testing out new ways of living.

We all have particular viewpoints on what is important when it comes to grieving – how long one should spend processing the loss, and how soon one should focus on building a new life. You might feel impatient with yourself and feel you should be moving on; and/or you might feel pressure from others to deal with the change instead of continuing to grieve; or, you might feel you need to stay in the past and be reluctant to engage with change.

Whatever you are experiencing, it is important to keep in mind that both *processing the past* and *taking steps to deal with the change* and move forward are important. Both have their place and will be useful to you while working through your grief. If you only engage in processing your past loss and never engage with your "new reality" and the change process, you are likely to end up feeling depressed and experience little joy in your current life. However, if you were only focusing on change and moving on, you are also likely going to feel unhappy in the future. Your unprocessed grief and the attached emotions will show up when you least expect it and will likely make it difficult for you to feel truly happy and content in life, regardless of how well you did building your new life.

THE PROCESS OF ADAPTING TO CHANGE

The process of change involves:

- Grieving and accepting the loss you have experienced
- Addressing your difficulties and resistance to change
- Developing new skills
- Making important changes to adapt to your new reality
- Exploring opportunities and positives in your new role

Once this process is complete, it usually takes a while to completely settle into your new reality and feel that you can fully engage with the positives the change has brought and embrace your new reality.

Looking at the necessary steps that make up the process of change, you might notice that you have already engaged with most aspects by working through this book so far.

- You will have already made great progress with grieving and accepting your loss by completing chapters 4 to 7.
- You have also started to look at your difficulties with change (for example, learning to accept difficult feelings without engaging in avoidance in chapter 5).
- You have also already taken important steps to adapt to your new reality in chapter 3.
- Making changes and learning new skills will be ongoing as you continue to use the insights and techniques in this book.

This chapter will further help you to increase your confidence in coping with change and address any difficulties you are experiencing.

You might have started to appreciate that the process of change is not as linear and neat as you might have imagined; that it is normal to move from one process to the next and back again, or work on two processes at the same time. Again, there is no right or wrong way of how to move through the grieving process. People usually find it helpful to mainly focus on dealing with the loss, then address difficulties and resistances, before finally devoting the most energy and resources to developing new skills and adapting fully to change in the final stages of the grieving process. In reality, you will of course be needing to adapt to changes from the start to some degree. Likewise, it is common to find yourself in the final stages of adapting to your new life when an event or situation will trigger you to feel your grief more intensely again; this will then require you to go back and do some further processing or reflecting on what has been lost.

DIFFICULTIES WITH CHANGE

Having difficulties with change, and perhaps not wanting to change at all, is completely normal and understandable after a significant loss. There are various reasons why we can find it difficult to cope with change, but one of the main reasons is that change can feel very overwhelming and uncertain. It is a self-protective mechanism to avoid anything that makes you feel you cannot cope, especially when you are already not feeling as confident and strong as you normally might. Engaging in change involves taking some risks and exposing yourself to potential failure and further disappointment, which understandably might be the last thing you want to experience at the moment!

Let's look at the difficulties Paddy, Monica and Susan experienced with change to help you start to think about your own difficulties with change.

PADDY'S STORY

Paddy went through a terrible divorce, which left him feeling bitter and hopeless about how he was ever going to feel joyful again. The divorce meant that financially he was suddenly years behind what he had worked toward, and he was no longer able to live the life he used to. He tried to be a good father, but found it challenging at times to have the relationship he wanted with his sons and make it how it used to be. He wanted to be happy again. He started to date soon after leaving the family home, hoping he would find a woman who would appreciate him and love him for who he was. However, as soon as women showed an interest in getting to know him better, he would find reasons to stop seeing them. When he reflected on what was happening, he realized that a deep mistrust and fear of being taken advantage of was getting triggered – which was just how he felt toward his ex-wife. He also noticed that getting closer to someone made him sad, as it reminded him of how he felt he had lost the close relationship he had with his boys, which he found very painful to face. Paddy realized that in order to be able to adapt to his new reality and find a new partner he was able to trust, he needed to spend more time grieving what he had lost and process how this had affected him emotionally, otherwise these emotions would always get in the way of him building a new, satisfying relationship.

MONICA'S STORY

Monica was made redundant from her job as a researcher at a university. While she had been unhappy in her job for years, it was still a shock for her to find out that she had to leave her job. What she struggled with most was the prospect of having to go through the process of finding a new job. She had to decide whether to pursue another job in academia, which was likely to lead to her having to face the same challenges again, or whether to change her career and possibly even retrain. Monica was someone who generally found it difficult to believe in herself, and was used to working in academia. The prospect of having to make a choice and take the risk of deciding how to proceed, applying for jobs and potentially having to learn new skills, terrified her. She was worried about making the wrong choice, being unable to adjust to a new environment, and coping with all the potential rejections along the way. When Monica talked about her difficulties with a friend who had gone through something similar, she realized that her fears were probably quite normal and to be expected. She also noticed that what she needed was to get a good support system in place to help her make new connections, and that it was possible to learn new skills that would help her find a new job. She realized that adapting to her new situation would take time, and that coping with rejection and temporary "failings" along the way was something that she would need to learn come to terms with. She started to feel that perhaps she was able to cope with the change with the help of friends and family.

SUSAN'S STORY

Susan lost her mum two years ago, having cared for her for years while she was suffering from terminal breast cancer. Susan had always been close to her mum, and caring for her had brought them even closer. While she had felt some relief for her mum and for herself when her mother finally found peace, she also found it difficult to find any new enjoyment in her life. Grieving her mother had been a difficult process, and had understandably taken a long time and was still ongoing; but while the intensity of the feelings of sadness, anger and guilt about her loss reduced over time, Susan nevertheless felt quite depressed and increasingly hopeless about her life. She felt lost about the extra time she suddenly had available, and felt no interest in anything. She had expected that she would finally be able to do and enjoy all the things she had been unable to do while caring for her mum, and did not understand why she no longer felt like doing any of them. When reflecting on what was getting in her way with her therapist, they noticed that she had a strong belief that moving on with her life would be disrespectful toward her mum, and would mean she no longer cared about having lost her. She feared that creating new meaningful relationships and engaging in new roles might make her feel less close to her mum and that she would slowly forget about her. Together with her therapist, Susan looked at her beliefs and what was useful and not so useful about them, and what effect holding on to those beliefs had on her depression and quality of life. Susan decided that she wanted to let go of her old beliefs and find newer, more realistic and helpful beliefs, which she did. She then felt ready to explore the positives about her new life, and started making plans to meet up with friends she had meant to contact for a long time, as well as deciding to take up hiking again, which she had enjoyed in the past.

ADDRESSING YOUR DIFFICULTIES

To find out which areas of change you are struggling with, it is helpful to ask yourself what might be useful or good about not engaging in the process of change. Your initial reaction might be that there is *nothing* good about not engaging in the process of change – and if you are in the process of adapting and responding to your new reality, you are probably doing really well and you can skip the rest of this chapter!

However, if you can feel a resistance to engaging with the process of change as a result of your loss, there must be at least a part of you that feels that there is a good reason for not wanting to adapt!

If I were to have asked Paddy what was good about not embracing his new reality (grieving his losses) before he realized what was going on, he might have said that it was good that he would not have to face all the difficult feelings in relation to his many losses as a result of the end of his marriage. Monica might have said that by resisting adapting to her new situation she was able to protect herself from possible disappointment and failure. And Susan might have said that not engaging in the process of change was showing deep respect for her mum and helping her to maintain a deep emotional connection. It's understandable why all three felt some resistance to change at the beginning. However, the key is that the beliefs they held about what was good about "not engaging in the change process" were not 100 per cent true. For example, Monica was right that by not applying for new jobs or retraining she could possibly avoid further disappointment and failure, but by not doing so and staying unemployed, she would most definitely end up feeling she had failed – and be disappointed with herself and the situation indefinitely.

The key to working with resistance to change is that you don't have to completely let go of your beliefs that are holding you back, but it is always useful to adjust their strength to a level that is helpful. For example, after talking with her friend and seeing things more clearly, Monica decided that she wanted to adapt the strength of her belief that "not applying for new jobs could avoid further disappointment and failure" from 85 per cent to 30 per cent. This was enough to allow her to feel positive and determined enough to start applying for some jobs, while still being able to hold on to the belief to some extent.

When dealing with internal resistance, there is often a good (and usually protective) reason why we hold on strongly to a certain belief. Trying to change it or get rid of it completely usually only leads to more resistance, while reducing its strength often feels easier and lowers resistance.

EXERCISE
Identifying and Reducing Your Difficulties with Change

1. Draw your awareness to what you are currently finding difficult about the process of change and adapting to your new reality. Notice any feelings, especially feelings of resistance.
   Example: Panic, feeling like looking away.

2. Ask yourself what might be good about not engaging in the process of change and adapting to your new reality. Write down all thoughts and beliefs that come to your mind. Keep going until you cannot find any more.
   Example: Not engaging in change (grieving my losses) will stop me from feeling overwhelmed. Not making the effort to try a new relationship will stop me feeling deeply disappointed and alone again.

3. Rate the strength of each belief from 0 to 100 per cent. Acknowledge the importance of and what is good about holding these beliefs.
   Example: Not engaging in change (grieving my losses) will stop me from feeling overwhelmed. 90 per cent. Not making the effort to try a new relationship will stop me from feeling deeply disappointed and alone again. 75 per cent.

4. Then ask yourself what strength (from 0 to 100 per cent) you would like the belief to be, and what you feel would be helpful going forward. Perhaps you are starting to see that the belief is not as valid as you initially thought it was? Do you feel you need to reassess how helpful holding on to this belief so strongly really is? Be completely honest with yourself, and only decide on reducing its strength by as much as you feel comfortable with for now.

Example: Not engaging in change (grieving my losses) will stop me from feeling overwhelmed. 35 per cent. Not making the effort to try a new relationship will stop me from feeling deeply disappointed and alone again. 45 per cent.

5. Draw your awareness back to what you are currently finding difficult about your new reality and the change you are going through. Notice how you feel about it now. Do you feel any less resistant and more positive about engaging with it now?

6. Make a note of any insights and learning.

Difficulties with the process of change usually fall into one of three categories: past, present, future. Apart from addressing your beliefs that stop you from engaging with your new reality, it will also be important for you to focus on tasks and exercises specific to either the past, present or future (depending on which you most struggle with), as they will help you with resolving your resistance.

Below you will find a table listing the difficulties with change one can experience relating to the past, present or future and the solutions that will help to overcome them.

DIFFICULTIES WITH CHANGE		
PAST	**PRESENT**	**FUTURE**
Not having grieved what you have lost enough in order to be able to focus on the present and the future without getting triggered too frequently or intensely by your loss.	Fears about not being able to cope with, or failing the process of, change and adjusting to your new reality.	Concerns and fears about your new reality, and therefore resisting engaging with it.

SOLUTIONS		
PAST	**PRESENT**	**FUTURE**
Revisit the areas of your past – and the emotions – that still need processing. Be patient and generous with yourself and the time it takes for you to feel better. Go back to your notes from chapters 4 to 7 and repeat the exercises you are most drawn to or that you found most helpful. Challenge your belief that engaging with difficult feelings will make things worse or is pointless. Remember that the more we try to fight feelings, the stronger they become. Challenge your concerns and fears about your new reality using the exercise on page 142.	Implement the exercises and tasks in the remainder of this chapter, including setting SMART goals, learning new skills, setting up new routines and drawing on old or new support systems. Challenge your belief of not being able to cope and/or failing. Remember that feeling somewhat insecure or negative about the process is completely normal! The key is to not let it overwhelm you. Challenge your concerns and fears about your new reality using the exercise on page 142.	Challenge your concerns and fears about your new reality using the exercise on page 142. How helpful is it to have these concerns and fears, and do you overestimate how valid they are? What is the evidence? How much would you like to let go of your concerns and fears? What will your future look like if you will continue to believe in your fears and concerns as strongly as you do right now? Look at the benefits of your new reality – what are the possible opportunities or positives?

Looking at the last table, I would like you to go back to the beliefs you identified in the last exercise. For each belief, determine whether this indicates a difficulty with change in the category of past, present or future. It will give you a good indication of which areas you still need to focus on and how best to spend your time to make progress.

ADAPTING TO AND EMBRACING YOUR NEW REALITY

Getting used to and feeling comfortable and secure in your new reality takes time, and will feel uncomfortable sometimes. However, if you do engage with it, new opportunities and possibilities will open up, and you will find happiness, excitement and hope again. To fully adapt to your new reality, you will need to address the practical challenges of settling into your new role and explore what your new reality might have to offer.

INCREASING YOUR CONFIDENCE

One of the most difficult challenges about your new reality will be that you are suddenly asked to do things that you might not have done before or do not feel confident in. To help with this, it will be important for you to identify the skills you need to learn (or relearn) and the areas you need to increase your confidence in. It might seem daunting at first, but once you have identified them, you can work on each – step by step – and they will soon feel less overwhelming.

After losing her job, Monica realized she needed to:

- *Improve her networking skills to increase her chances of finding a new job, especially as she was interested in changing careers.*
- *Improve her job interviewing skills.*
- *Develop skills to deal with rejection and disappointment.*
- *Learn to believe in herself more.*

Monica also realized that many of the skills she had developed as a researcher would help her with researching and deciding on a career path and finding suitable courses.

She also felt that involving friends and talking with people from different industries would help her to explore and decide on a new career.

EXERCISE
Identifying New Skills

1. What are the tasks you need to do, and new difficulties you are facing, since experiencing your loss? Which ones do you keep putting off, or avoid completely, or feel very anxious about?
2. What skills do you need in order to address these tasks and difficulties?
3. If you are not sure which skills you need, who or what could help you to better understand what you will need?
4. Which of your existing skills will help you to learn new skills and overcome your difficulties? Make sure you list each of your valuable skills and elaborate on how they will be useful in your current situation.

Now that you have identified the new skills you need, the skills you already have, and ways you can find out which skills you will need if you are unsure, I want you to use this information to create an action plan. Remember, we will be taking things step by step, and you can work at the pace that feels right for you.

To ensure you are setting an action plan that will be achievable and will help you to see your successes quickly and efficiently, I want you to set yourself SMART goals for each identified new skill.

SMART stands for:

- **Specific** – be specific about your goal/sub-goal and the skill you want to learn.
- **Measurable** – how will you track your progress?
- **Achievable** – is the goal achievable and realistic with the resources available to you?
- **Relevant** – is your goal/sub-goal relevant to achieving your overall goal and life plan?
- **Time-bound** – what is your target date for completing your goal/sub-goal?

If the new skill is something that will likely take a long time to acquire or require a lot of effort and time, I want you to break down learning the new skill into several SMART goals. It's usually best to start with smaller goals and work your way through them, rather than going for a big goal that will take a lot of time to achieve and may make you lose motivation and focus.

EXERCISE
Setting SMART Goals

1. For each new skill you identify, decide how many sub-goals it should be broken down into. Try to break them down so the time to complete each sub-goal is one month or less. You can set bigger goals as you move along and once you get used to the process. *Example: Improve job interviewing skills. Sub-goals: 1. Read book on job interviewing skills and complete all relevant exercises. 2. Practise job interviews with others.*
2. For each skill identified, start with the first sub-goal and define this as a SMART goal.

Example: Improve job interviewing skills. Research/ buy book on job interviewing skills/techniques. Read book and complete relevant exercises for at least eight hours each week. I would like to have completed this task within four weeks.

3. Action your first SMART goal and track your progress.
4. Once you have completed your first SMART goal, move on to the next sub-goal and repeat steps 2 and 3 above until you have learnt your new skill!
5. If you find yourself struggling to complete your SMART goal, redefine it using the prompts above. It's common for people to set unachievable goals, be unrealistic about the time it takes to complete a goal, or underestimate the resources needed. Don't worry when this happens – use it as a learning experience.

EXPLORING POSITIVES AND OPPORTUNITIES

It will be really beneficial for you to look at the positives and opportunities your new situation has to offer. It can be really difficult to think of positives, and you might be convinced that there are none! This is completely understandable. You might also feel that any positives or values you *could* potentially identify have no value to you at present.

Allow yourself to think of at least a few possible opportunities or positives that could come from your loss. Sometimes, the very step of just allowing yourself to explore what positives there could be helps your mind to shift from a place where you feel stuck and hopeless to a place where change and positivity seem possible again. It's okay if you still feel attached to what you have lost and don't want to accept your new reality just yet, but there may be a tiny bit of you that feels okay to open yourself up to the possibility of change.

SUSAN'S STORY

After Susan lost her mum, she initially found it really difficult to find any positives about her new reality. She did not feel like engaging with anything, and spent a lot of time thinking about her mum and how much she missed her.

After exploring with her therapists what was making Susan so resistant to change, she was willing to look at some positives and opportunities. She said that other people might appreciate the spare time she now had, and that she should feel good about having time to spend time with friends, as well as having time to date again, as she had "put off" doing this while she cared for her mum.

The therapists asked her what might be good about doing enjoyable things with friends, and dating again. Susan said that this might make her feel more connected and "alive" again, and that she might benefit from talking to others about how she felt. She also said that dating might help her find a close relationship and this could help her to feel less lonely.

They continued to look at all the possible positives and opportunities in more detail. At the end of their exploration, Susan still felt somewhat apprehensive about fully embracing her new reality. However, she felt a lot less fearful and more hopeful about how doing so could actually benefit her. Together with her therapists, she tentatively set herself some SMART goals around contacting and making arrangements for dinner with two of her friends and joining a local hiking club.

EXERCISE
Exploring Positives and Opportunities Your New Reality has to Offer

1. Jot down any positives or opportunities your new reality might possibly have to offer. Write down anything that comes to mind, even if you are not completely convinced by it or you are not sure if the positive holds any value for you at this moment in time. Imagine what you would say to someone else who was in your situation.

2. Explore each positive/opportunity in more detail. What exactly is good about the positive/opportunity? How could it benefit you, and which positive feelings might it create for you? Allow yourself to really imagine what life *could* be like if you were to engage with the positives and opportunities.

3. Take the positives/opportunities that feel most appealing to you and set yourself two (or more) SMART goals that will lead you toward them.

4. Continue reviewing how you feel about your positives/opportunities, and set new SMART goals as you go along, until you notice yourself naturally taking steps to embrace your new reality and it no longer feels difficult to do so.

SOCIAL SUPPORT SYSTEMS

Throughout this book, I mention how important and crucial a good support system is when going through any emotional difficulties. Likewise, adapting to and coping with change makes us feel vulnerable and out of our depth; it is the support and encouragement from others that often help us to keep going, and able to face what we would otherwise find too frightening. Using a good social support system is a key strategy to successfully cope with change.

If you are finding that you do not have enough support around you, go back to chapter 3 to find tips and strategies to rebuild your social support. Remember that there are many online support groups and forums, as well as local support groups, which are usually easy to join. These will help you to connect with others who are also coping with change.

REVIEWING YOUR GOALS AND BELIEFS ABOUT YOURSELF

Please update the ratings of your goals and the beliefs about yourself in relation to your loss. Your ratings are likely to have changed quite a bit since chapter 4. All the work and effort you have put in to dealing with your loss is surely paying off! We will be reviewing your ratings again in chapter 15. By then, you will likely have started to learn new skills, have put some of your SMART goals into action, and increased your confidence in embracing your new reality.

TRACKING YOUR GOALS AND PROGRESS

Date:

Rate on a scale of 1–10 to what extent you feel you have already reached these goals, where 1 means not at all and 10 means completely:

My first goal is: _____

Rating: /10

My second goal is: _____

Rating: /10

My third goal is: _____

Rating: /10

Negative belief: _____

Right now, how disturbing does it feel to think of the worst part/moment of your loss and the negative belief about yourself? Rate on a scale of 0–10, where 0 means no disturbance at all and 10 means the most disturbance you can imagine.

Rating: /10

Positive belief: _____

How true does the positive statement feel to you right now when you think about your loss? Rate on a scale of 1–10, where 1 means not true at all and 10 means completely true.

Rating: /10

CHAPTER SUMMARY

- It's normal to find coping with and adapting to change difficult, especially after having experienced a major loss.
- Every loss leads to change, so adapting to change is an essential part of the grieving process.
- It's helpful to be aware of the multitude of losses you have experienced already and the changes you coped with successfully.
- The process of change is non-linear, and is continuously happening throughout your grieving process. You will find your unique balance between when to focus on processing your loss and when to focus on coping with current change.
- Identifying your individual difficulties with change, reviewing the validity of your beliefs around change, and engaging with activities that specifically address your difficulties will help you to reduce your resistance to and increase your confidence in coping with change.
- Embracing your new reality includes increasing your confidence by learning new skills, making important changes in your life, and exploring positives and opportunities.
- Becoming comfortable and secure in your new reality takes time, and will feel uncomfortable sometimes. However, if you do engage with change, new opportunities and possibilities will open up and you will find happiness, excitement and hope again.

9

YOUR MENTAL HEALTH

This book has been written for those who struggle to grieve their loss. It is very likely that if you have been experiencing difficulties with how to cope with your loss, you will have also experienced some signs of depression and anxiety. As we have covered throughout this book, it is a normal reaction to feel sad, anxious, angry, overwhelmed or panicked, and to experience emotions that might be unfamiliar to you. Nevertheless, there are instances when the way you feel, and your experiences and behaviours, might indicate that you are suffering from a mental health condition, and would perhaps benefit from further professional support.

This chapter provides a brief overview of the different mental health disorders that are most likely to occur alongside, or as a direct result of, difficulties with grieving your loss. In addition, there are situations and signs, which I will also outline, that I would highly recommend you respond to by seeking professional advice and support. Familiarizing yourself with these signs and symptoms will help to guide you in the right direction and empower you to make the right decisions for yourself if needed.

SUICIDAL IDEATION AND RISK-TAKING

Persistent thoughts and ideations about dying or how to take your life, and wanting to act on these thoughts or even having put a plan in place of how to end your life.

This includes engaging in actions that put your life at risk, even if you might not have actively thought of the risk at that time, and persistent fantasizing about joining the person you lost, and seeing this as a realistic option to help end your suffering.

You are generally also at a higher risk of suicide if there are others in your family who have taken their life.

ADDICTION

Using alcohol, drugs or any other addictive behaviours or substances excessively to numb your pain and cope with your emotions.

While you are using substances or engaging in addictive behaviours, most emotional coping strategies and techniques will be a lot less effective, as the addiction will continue to affect your mental health negatively and cause difficulties such as anxiety, shame, relationship problems and depression. You will need to get your problem use or behaviours under control before you can tackle any of your other difficulties. Addictions are far too powerful for anyone to address on their own.

DIFFICULTY WITH DAY-TO-DAY FUNCTIONING

Struggling with day-to-day activities and finding it hard to return to some of your usual routines and normal functioning after a month has passed since your loss.

It's normal to take a long time to *completely* return to feeling yourself again and functioning in all areas; but if you are struggling with basic routines, such as sleep, leaving your home, shopping and feeding yourself adequately, for more than a month – and this is not due to any physical health problems or limitations – you will likely benefit from professional support.

Similarly, if you are struggling to return to work or education after six months have passed, professional help would be useful. Of course, it is beneficial to take as much time off work or your studies as you need to process your grief, and the time you will need completely depends on the kind of loss you have experienced. However, once a certain time has passed, being off work or your studies can also have a negative effect on your mental health and self-esteem.

MENTAL HEALTH CONDITIONS

In general, being diagnosed with a mental health condition relates to the severity and the length of time you have experienced certain emotions, thoughts or problems. You might have experienced quite a few of the symptoms and diagnostic criteria of most mental health conditions, but you would only be diagnosed with a mental health disorder once you have met the criteria for a particular period of time and they have caused you significant distress and impairment. In addition, diagnoses such as generalized anxiety and depression affect everyone slightly differently, and symptoms can range from mild to severe. when deciding whether to seek help, it's important to take the severity of your symptoms into account.

If your symptoms have been severe over a considerable amount of time, I would strongly suggest seeing a medical professional to assess your mental health and advise on effective treatment options.

Battling it all on your own is impossible, and your friends and family might feel out of their depth in trying to support you adequately when your symptoms are severe.

If, after reading this chapter, you suspect you might have a mental health condition but your symptoms are in the mild or medium range, by no means do you need to seek immediate professional help, unless you wish to, of course. Using the self-care techniques in this book and the exercises to cope with and accept your emotions, as well as identifying and working through areas that keep you stuck, will all help you to reduce your symptoms. However, you might want to take into account how long you have had your symptoms, how easy or difficult it has been for you to feel better by using the techniques and exercises in this book, and how much your symptoms impair you.

If your symptoms have been there for a long time and not shifted very much, even though you have attempted to work on your difficulties, and you feel this has been affecting your quality of life or social and general functioning, you might well benefit from professional medical or therapeutic support.

Depending on the country you live in, your first point of contact will either be your primary care physician or another medical professional who will be qualified to assess your mental health, give you evidence-based advice regarding treatment, and refer you to appropriate specialist services or a psychiatrist. You can, of course, also choose to see a therapist or a psychologist if you feel more comfortable with seeking psychological rather than medical help. However, please be aware that, depending on whether you see a psychotherapist, psychologist or counsellor, and depending on which country you live in, these professionals are less likely to be able to offer you a firm diagnosis.

Here is a list of mental health conditions that can either be triggered by a major loss or can be experienced alongside your grief. This list is by no means exhaustive, and the descriptions are given as guidelines only to help you identify any problems you might be experiencing. If you are concerned about any symptoms or experiences, please do see your primary care physician, who will either be able to offer you the right support or put your mind at rest.

DEPRESSION

The common feature of all depressive disorders is the presence of sadness, emptiness or irritable moods, together with somatic and cognitive changes that significantly affect the sufferer's ability to function. The most common form of depression is clinically referred to as "major depressive disorder".

A **major depressive disorder** is defined as experiencing at least five of the following symptoms for more than two weeks (including at least one of the symptoms in bold):[13]

- **Feeling sad, empty or hopeless**
- **Reduced interest or pleasure in most activities**
- Significant weight gain or loss
- Sleeping too much or too little
- Being restless or slowed down
- Loss of energy
- Feeling worthless or excessively guilty
- Reduced ability to think or concentrate or being markedly indecisive
- Recurrent thoughts of suicide

There are other forms of depression, such as **persistent depressive disorder** (dysthymia) and **specified depressive disorders**, which are similar to major depressive disorder, but differ in the severity, length and amount of symptoms that need to be present to meet their criteria.

ANXIETY

Anxiety disorders share the experience of "excessive" fear and anxiety and related behavioural disturbances, including avoidance behaviours; "excessive" means that the level of anxiety or fear is disproportionate to the threat level and what would be expected developmentally. Anxiety disorders differ from one another in the types of objects or situations that induce anxiety and the associated cognitive thought processes.

Generalized anxiety disorder is defined as experiencing excessive fear and worry about a number of events or activities on most days for at least six months.[14] People with this diagnosis find it difficult to control their worry, and their worry often jumps from one subject to another, hardly ever leaving them worry-free. In addition, the anxiety and worry occurs with at least three of the following symptoms:

- Feeling restless or on edge
- Being easily fatigued
- Difficulty concentrating or mind going blank
- Irritability
- Muscle tension
- Sleep disturbances

Social anxiety disorder (social phobia) is marked by fear and anxiety about social situations during which the sufferer is expecting to be negatively judged by others and feel embarrassed/humiliated. The individual often worries about displaying anxiety symptoms and behaviours in these situations that will be visible to others and negatively evaluated. Often people will either avoid the feared social situations or endure them with intense anxiety and by using safety behaviours. The symptoms must have been present for at least six months before diagnosis.

Panic attacks can occur alongside any anxiety disorder or trauma-related disorders, and are abrupt surges of intense fear or intense discomfort, which can be expected or unexpected. The fear is usually experienced as physical symptoms, such as heart-pounding, shaking, nausea, shortness of breath and feeling dizzy, as well as anxious thoughts about the meaning of the panic attack (for example, losing control or having a mental breakdown, having a heart attack or dying). They are a result of heightened anxiety. Persistent worry and catastrophizing about panic attacks, and going to great lengths to avoid situations that might trigger an attack, is known as **panic disorder**.

TRAUMA- AND STRESSOR-RELATED DISORDERS

Trauma- and stressor-related disorders are disorders that develop in response to a traumatic or stressful event. Our brain is usually very skilled at dealing with stressful and even traumatic events, but there are certain external and internal factors that can hinder natural trauma-processing and lead to long-term difficulties. The nature and severity of the trauma are, of course, also important factors.

Prolonged grief disorder is defined as a pervasive grief response in reaction to the death of a person close to the patient.[15] It is characterized by longing for the deceased and persistent preoccupation with the deceased, as well as meeting the following criteria:

- The experience of intense emotions in relation to the death, which may include or lead to:
  o pain, anger, sadness, blame, numbness
  o denial or difficulty accepting the death
  o inability to experience positive emotions
  o difficulties in engaging with social or other activities

- The grief response persists for an atypically long period of time following the loss (at least six months), and clearly exceeds expected social, cultural or religious norms.
- The symptoms cause significant impairment in important areas of function (such as personal, social, educational or occupational).

Post-traumatic stress disorder (PTSD) is defined as meeting all of the following criteria for more than one month:[16]

- Having been exposed to actual or threatened death, serious injury or sexual violence.
- Experiencing one or more intrusion symptoms associated with the traumatic event, such as:
  - involuntary and distressing memories
  - flashbacks
  - intense psychological and/or physiological distress at exposure to internal or external cues
- Persistent avoidance of thoughts, feelings, memories about the traumatic event, or reminders
- Experiencing at least two negative changes in cognitions and mood as a result of the traumatic event, such as:
  - inability to remember an important aspect of the traumatic event
  - persistent and exaggerated negative beliefs or expectations about oneself or others
  - feeling detached from others
- Changes in arousal and reactivity associated with the traumatic event, such as:
  - irritable or aggressive behaviour
  - hypervigilance
  - sleep disturbance

It is important to note that PTSD is only diagnosed when the above symptoms are experienced for longer than one month. For shorter periods (three days up to a month) of experiencing significant distress and impairment after a traumatic event, the diagnosis of **acute stress disorder** is used.

Adjustment disorder is defined as experiencing behavioural and emotional reactions to an identifiable stressor and meeting all of the following criteria:

- Significant distress in response to the stressor that is objectively out of proportion to the severity or intensity of the stressor, leading to significant impairment in important areas of function (such as occupational or social functioning).
- The symptoms do not represent emotional or behavioural reactions that would be expected during bereavement.
- The symptoms persist for more than six months after the stressor or its consequences have ended.

SEEK HELP IF YOU ARE:

- Experiencing persistent suicidal thoughts and ideations, especially if you have acted on, or feel you want to act on, these thoughts.
- Depending on substances or addictive behaviours to cope with your emotions or numb your pain.
- Continuing to struggle with day-to-day activities and are finding it hard to return to some of normal functioning after a month has passed since you experienced your loss.
- Suspecting you might suffer from a mental health condition and your symptoms have been medium to severe.
- Experiencing persistent symptoms that have not shifted very much even though you have attempted to work on your difficulties, and this has been affecting your quality of life or social and general functioning.

PART 2

SPECIFIC EVENTS LEADING TO LOSS AND GRIEF

10

BEREAVEMENT

This chapter is written specifically for those who have experienced a bereavement. If this applies to you, you will benefit from reading this chapter in conjunction with the first eight chapters of this book as they contain further specific insight, advice and exercises to support you and guide you in your grieving process.

WHAT YOU EXPERIENCE WHEN A PERSON CLOSE TO YOU DIES

Many people will find that the experience of a person close to them dying is the most difficult loss one can experience. If you have lost someone who was a significant part of your life and they are suddenly gone, you may feel like your life has fallen to pieces. Sometimes, you might feel like you are drowning in all the emotion and the pain that seems never-ending. You might find it difficult to know how to react and what to do. Depending on who you lost and how important they were in your life, your process of grieving will have its particular challenges.

Your grief might pull you down deeper and deeper, but there will come a time when you have a choice about whether you want to remain heavily weighted by your despair, or whether you want to find fulfilment and meaning in your life again. Of course, it takes time, and there is no rush.

Death causes us to feel a deep sense of pain, often both emotionally and physically. The pain you feel is caused by the immense emotional investment you had in the person. Often this means the intense love you felt for that person; but other times the emotions might be more complex and include anger or disappointment, which can cause just as much pain. Feeling the pain is a necessary part of remembering the person you have lost. Pining or yearning for a close person who has died is another common experience. You probably wish that they would just come back, or that you could magically turn back time. You might find it impossible to believe that you will never again be able to speak to, see, touch or sense the person you have lost.

It's common to feel very lonely during the initial stages of grief. Sometimes it seems as if no one understands and, as time passes, you might feel that other people have returned to their "normal" lives, while you are still in the depth of your grieving. With time, the feeling of loneliness will diminish and you will start to feel ready to connect to those around you again. However, it is completely normal for there to be a period of time when all you can think or care about is the person who died.

After a person dies, it is in our nature to look at the causes and, ultimately, to apportion blame. The person who might be blamed might be a doctor or another relative, but very often, we direct the blame at ourselves. You may wonder whether there was something you should have done to prevent the death, or at least delay it. You might give yourself a hard time for not doing enough, or something particular, for the person while they were still alive. Our need to identify causes and review what could have prevented something bad from happening is natural, and often a very useful skill; but when it comes to someone dying, we often take on exaggerated self-blame that is driven by our powerlessness over death. As we are so used to taking responsibility, and have made such great advances as human beings, it's difficult to come to terms with the fact that maybe nothing we could have done would have stopped the person dying or made their death less painful – death happens. It's never a singular reason that causes someone's death, but many factors coming together. Blaming yourself is not going to change what happened and as much as you might want to believe otherwise, you are and always will be – as well as everyone else is – still very powerless when it comes to death.

Once the first intense phase of grieving has passed, the pain, loneliness and other difficult feelings will lessen, and you will slowly engage with your life again. Life may no longer be the same as it was before, but it's your life nevertheless – a life that deserves to be valued and cared for. With time, you will have longer periods of not feeling consumed by grief, and of feeling more like yourself again. No one can tell you how long the process will take as it is completely unique to you.

Many people will get to a place where they enjoy life again and are able to remember the person who they have lost with gratitude and love, or are no longer upset about any unresolved issues. It's important not to put pressure on yourself to get to this place. In fact, some people – for their own personal reasons – have made peace with never getting there. Many parents who have lost a child, for example, might remain in a place where they can feel okay for long periods of time and engage in a fulfilled life, but they might also have times when they continue to struggle to come to terms with their loss. Everyone is unique – as long as you are okay with where you are, no one can tell you otherwise.

Before we move on to the next part of this chapter, take a moment to check in with yourself about whether you feel you need any further understanding or knowledge about what you are going through while grieving. If you do, go back to chapters 1 and 2.

HOW YOU CAN SUPPORT YOUR OWN GRIEVING PROCESS

I encourage you to follow and use each exercise in chapters 3 to 8, as these will help immensely in your grieving process. In addition, here are some pointers about which areas to pay particular attention to and some additional tips and advice.

- **Describe your loss** (chapter 4). The person who died might have taken on many roles in your life, and it will help your understanding to be aware of all the areas that are affected by your loss. It will help you to break things down and grieve each aspect on its own, rather than feeling overwhelmed from trying to grieve all at once.
- **Identify the negative belief** you have about yourself in relation to having lost a person close to you, and the **positive belief** you would rather hold about yourself instead (chapter 4). Keep holding the positive belief in mind and review the strength of your negative and positive beliefs throughout your grieving process.
- **Identify and become more accepting of the feelings you are uncomfortable with** (chapter 5). Some of your feelings might be new, unexpected, overwhelming or deeply upsetting. Helping you to accept them will make it less of a struggle for you to go through your grieving process.
- **Write a letter to the person you have lost** (chapter 5). This will help you to get in touch with your emotions; expressing what you might have wanted to say to the person, but were unable to, will help you to resolve some emotions.
- **Create a detailed timeline of your loss** (chapter 6). Create your own story.
- **Tell your story** (chapter 7). You might have to/want to tell this many times – there is no limit, as long as you are finding it helpful with finding answers and processing feelings.

- **Remember the relationship you have lost in a balanced way**. Balance is crucial to be able to grieve the person fully, with all their good and more challenging sides. There is no need to hide anything. Grieving only part of the person will make it difficult to fully make peace with your loss.
- **Challenge the thoughts and beliefs that keep you stuck** (chapter 7). Any repetitive thought/belief that makes you feel very upset or down is likely one that is unhelpful, and will benefit from being challenged.
- **Spiritual and faith aspects** can be very important in some people's grieving process. If you are spiritual or have a particular faith, you might find solace, answers, guidance and support from spiritual leaders and community groups, as well as from praying and taking part in rituals.

MAKING PEACE WITH DIFFICULT RELATIONSHIPS

Sometimes close relationships are not always straightforward, and when a person you had a difficult relationship with dies, grieving can be complicated. The finality of death will bring any hope of reconciliation, repair or justice to an end, which can feel unsettling, sad and painful. The feelings of anger, regret, guilt and deep sadness you had about the person and your relationship with them might dominate and make it difficult for you to grieve them. While you are no longer able to reconcile your complicated relationship directly, the good news is that you can still make peace with the aspects you found difficult, hated or feared about that person; doing so will lessen your difficult emotions toward them, and will allow you to grieve them instead of getting stuck in a circle of negative emotions. You don't have to forgive and forget completely, or let go of all the pain they have caused you, but you might be able to let go of just enough to allow you to move forward.

EXERCISE
Making Peace with Difficult Relationships

1. Describe what you found difficult about your relationship and the person.
2. Is there anything you miss/don't miss about that person?
3. Was there anything about the relationship you would have liked to have changed?
4. Which positive qualities did you like about the person?
5. What would you like to have said to the person about the difficulties you had with them?
6. What would you have like the person to have said back to you, and what would you have liked them to have done?
7. If step 5 and/or 6 feel difficult, who or what could have helped so you could have had a conversation that would feel like you were being understood and taken seriously? (i.e., a therapist, someone else explaining it to them, the person being in a different place or time when they were completely happy, etc.)
8. Imagine steps 5 to 7 and add or change anything until you feel everything has been expressed that needed to be said, and you feel your difficult feelings have decreased significantly. You should feel more relaxed and/or lighter and less troubled. You might notice that you will feel some sadness about how tragic your relationship has been, but this will come from a more compassionate place and will make you feel closer to the person, rather than having a hopeless quality and making you feel distant.
9. What image or memory would you like to hold on to

and take with you about that person? Make a note of the image/memory and anything else you learnt from this exercise.

FUNERALS AND MEMORIALS

Rituals, such as funerals and memorials to commemorate a person's life and grieve their death with wider family and the community, are immensely valuable. Expressing and witnessing grief together as a community, and creating and carrying out a ritual for the person who has died, acknowledges each person's grief and that of the community as a whole, and helps people to accept that the person is no longer alive. It is an opportunity to say goodbye and to celebrate the person's life, mark the end of a life and the beginning of a period of mourning and change. Telling the story of the person shows love, deep respect and appreciation, and reminds those present of seeing the person as a whole and puts the events around their death into perspective. If you are one of those who is grieving the deepest and has been closest to the person who has died, seeing others grieving with you and sharing their pain will provide you with a sense of relief that you do not have to go through this on your own. In fact, most people experience funerals and memorials as one of the few situations where they don't feel so alone with their grief and feel connected to others, therefore these events are crucial in everyone's grieving process.

There is something powerful about a ritual that is carried out in the community – it can help you get in touch with your emotions and move you through them in a way that nothing else does.

The format and order of service at a funeral or memorial is something very personal. It often follows what the person chose before their death, or what is believed would have been their choice. It can be a religious or non-religious service and might happen in a spiritual place or a natural burial ground. There is usually music the person would have chosen, speeches commemorating the person, and photos of the deceased on display. Often, a wake after the funeral or memorial can be a less formal way to talk and connect to others and to celebrate the person's life.

There are, of course, times when arranging a funeral or memorial service is difficult for a variety of reasons. However, it's important to remember how valuable these events are in helping everyone process their grief, and how it will help you. Many people find that not having a funeral or memorial can complicate and prolong grief, and you might struggle more if you were unable to attend the service or if there was none. I strongly suggest that you try your best to set up or create a memorial service that has meaning to you; you can invite as few or as many people as you like. If there are others that you feel might welcome this idea, it's probably useful to connect with them and set this up together, so you can offer each other support and feel more connected and valued.

HOW TO COPE WITH ANNIVERSARIES

Anniversaries of a person's death or their birthday can be particularly difficult and painful. It's important to support yourself as much as you can at these times, and use the days to remember the person's life and how important they were to you. Remember the person you have lost by doing something that is meaningful to you. Many people like to go somewhere or do something they enjoyed with the person they have lost. You could also invite mutual friends over for a meal and conversation, with each of you being able to share feelings or memories. You might want to light a candle or write a poem or letter to the person, or meditate while keeping the person and the love you feel for them in mind. You could give a donation to a charity that has meaning to you and the person.

It's usually best to have everything arranged well beforehand, as the day itself and even the days leading up to it might be very emotional and overwhelming. With a plan in place, it will be much easier to go through with, regardless of how you feel on the day; and you are likely to feel much better for it afterwards.

MAINTAINING A CONNECTION

When a person dies, it does not mean that you will completely lose that person, but your relationship with them will change. Their life will carry on through those who remember them and those whose life has been changed by their unique presence and influence.

Many people fear that they will forget their loved one. It's helpful to focus on the things you can do to remember them, rather than worrying about what you might forget. It is indeed possible and therapeutic to maintain a connection to the person who has died for as long and as intensely as feels right to you. Likewise, whenever you feel the need (or are ready) to spend less time thinking about them, that is absolutely fine too. Working out how you can stay connected with the person you have lost while also living your life might take a little time, and might also change over time. It will be entirely up to you how you would like to maintain your connection, but here are some suggestions.

- Create a memory book with photos of the person that have a special meaning to you, cards or letters you have received from them, anything you want to include from the funeral, stories with or about the person that you remember fondly, and any other items or keepsakes.
- Frame a favourite photo of both of you together and a photo of the person on their own.
- Talk to the person, either in your mind or out loud. Really engage with how you imagine they would respond. You can even ask them for advice or share what is going on in your life.
- Plant a flower or tree in memory of the person.
- Watch the person's favourite movies or listen to their favourite music.
- Donate to or volunteer for a charity that you feel would be valued by the person you have lost.
- Be kind and help others left behind by the person you lost, such as their children, partners/spouses or elderly parents.
- Ask others for their stories and memories and collect them in a book. You might be surprised what you will learn, and you will feel more connected to the person for it.
- Tell the story of the person who has died as often and to as many people as you like.
- Carry with you items that belonged to the person or photographs of them.
- Write down in your journal how you feel the person you lost has changed you and what you have learnt from them. What characteristics of the person were most valuable to you? Express your gratitude and joy for everything about them that enriched your life.

HOW YOU CAN FEEL POSITIVE ABOUT YOURSELF AND YOUR LIFE AGAIN

Depending on where you are in your grieving process, it might be too early to think about feeling positive about your life again. However, if you have been working through this book, you might feel ready to move on to engaging with some more positive feelings again.

You might be relieved to have learnt that grieving does not mean forgetting your loved one or having to carry on with your life without feeling their presence. Instead, what you might find is that you will create a different relationship with them, which is based on memory and legacy. As sad as it is that the person is no longer present with you in a physical sense, and you can no longer create new memories and experiences with them, what will always exist and live on are all the wonderful and valuable memories you shared. They will continue to live "within you" and within everyone else whose life they touched.

If you had a difficult or ambivalent relationship with the person who died, the way you might want to feel about them and how often you want to remember them after you have grieved their loss might be different. Instead of continuing to think about what upset you, you can find peace and learn to accept the person for who they were, with all their good and bad parts. It does not mean that you have to agree with what they have done, but you no longer have to spend energy wishing that things had been different or feeling angry and sad about it. If you find you are continuing to go over the same distressing feelings and memories, go back to previous chapters to help you explore what is stopping you from moving forward, as well as going back to the exercise earlier in this chapter on making peace with difficult relationships.

Someday, when you have worked through your grief and you feel you have spent enough time allowing yourself to feel and understand your loss – when you have addressed your blocks, hopes and fears – you will notice a feeling that tells you that it is time to step outside and leave your grieving behind, even if only temporarily to start with. It is likely to feel daunting, and you may not want to do it, but this will be the time when you have to take a leap of faith and learn to live again.

Whenever you decide to move on with your life after a period of mourning, it does not mean that you are forgetting or no longer value the person. Many people fear they are being disloyal if they enjoy life again after someone close to them has died. What I would like you to think about is what you believe the person you lost would have wanted for you, and how helpful it is to continue to keep your life on pause. You will probably find that they would have wanted you to feel happy again, and that they would have wanted you to continue and enjoy your life.

Feeling truly positive about yourself and your life again will take time. As humans we are meant to attach deeply, as well as being able to grieve losses and find new meaning and hope. Whoever you have lost is irreplaceable, and you don't have to replace them. You will learn to have new and different relationships with others, and with the person you have lost. You might find meaning in the time you had together and the meaning they had in your life, as well as you had in theirs. Your memories and the meaning you find in them will always live on.

11

INFERTILITY AND MISCARRIAGES

This chapter is written specifically for someone who has experienced a miscarriage, repeated miscarriages or is dealing with infertility. You will benefit from reading this chapter in conjunction with the first eight chapters of this book, as they contain further specific insight, advice and exercises to support you and guide you in your grieving process.

WHAT YOU EXPERIENCE AFTER A MISCARRIAGE AND WHEN YOU ARE DEALING WITH INFERTILITY

Both infertility and experiencing a miscarriage or repeated miscarriages are experienced as losses on a multitude of levels. On the surface, it is the loss of a baby – either the baby that one wished or expected to have, or the one that had already started to develop in the woman's womb. However, the meaning most attribute to their failure to reproduce effectively goes much deeper and, for many, defines how they see or value themselves as a person.

You might experience infertility or miscarriage as a loss of status as a man or woman, and a loss of purpose as a human being. You might also feel you lost your ability to create life either on your own or with your partner, and are therefore less valuable. Many find that they somehow feel broken or that there is something very wrong with them. You might start to doubt your value in your relationship, and struggle to feel as worthwhile as you used to, even if your partner assures you that their love for you remains the same. Some people, in a quest to make sense of why a miscarriage or infertility is happening to them, come to the conclusion that perhaps they do not deserve to have a baby and be as happy as others, or that they are being punished for something; somehow, they feel they must have caused the loss, or should at least have been able to prevent it from happening.

Many couples or individuals will also feel a huge sense of failure, and that somehow it is their fault that they are unable to conceive, especially if their diagnosis is one of "unexplained infertility". In their journey to get pregnant, they try to identify and fix any factors that might help them reach their goal – diet, supplements, spiritual healing or a range of psychological and physical treatments may be considered. When their infertility and struggles continue, they feel an even bigger sense of failure, as all their efforts do not seem enough or the right ones.

The truth is that you do deserve a baby. Miscarriages and infertility aren't anyone's fault and you are not broken. Nothing you have done or not done has caused this.

Couples and individuals can often feel very lonely when it comes to infertility and miscarriages. They find themselves as part of a club of that nobody wants to be a member of, yet once you are in it, it's difficult to escape. You might find it hard to share your grief with others, and you may try to avoid situations and people who remind you of your fertility struggles. Interacting with others who have children or found it easy to conceive might make you feel disconnected or remind you of your loss. Furthermore, their questions and comments can sometimes feel intrusive or insensitive, even if they come from a place of trying to be supportive.

Infertility can be particularly painful, as feelings of hope and excitement will continuously lead to feelings of pain, sadness and disappointment. Going through monthly menstrual cycles or rounds of IVF, only to experience repeated losses, can make you feel profoundly powerless, exhausted and helpless. You might become very frustrated with yourself and about not being able to make it happen, and become very self-critical, or overanxious and cautious about everything you do that could influence your chances of conceiving. You might also feel angry with those around you for not being more understanding and supportive, or with the apparent failure of medical professionals. The grieving can feel constant, and there never seems to be an end in sight as the possibility of conceiving continues to exist. How can one come to terms with a loss that never seems final?

Experiencing a miscarriage and the emotions felt immediately afterwards can be very intense and overwhelming. Most of the time, a miscarriage is unexpected and can lead to shock, panic, despair, as well as anger and guilt. Once the reality of it has fully settled in, the feelings of sadness, pain and emptiness often take over, and you might find it difficult to cope with everyday life. You might worry about conceiving and the possibility of miscarrying again, and fear you won't be able to cope with either. In addition to the emotional effects of a miscarriage, the physical effects should not be underestimated, and can often make it even more difficult for you to cope with your emotions and start to grieve your loss. You might feel drained, in pain or anxious about the symptoms caused by the miscarriage and the sudden shift of hormones or medical interventions needed. You might also feel exhausted for weeks on end. What you will need to remind yourself of is that your body, as well as your mind, deserves time to recover and to heal as it has been through a lot.

Every time a miscarriage is experienced or one experiences another failed attempt at conceiving, you will need to mourn the loss of the baby you imagined you would have, the loss of having a family or extending your family (in the traditional sense), and the loss of you becoming a mum or a dad and everything this entails for you. Conceiving and having a baby is deeply meaningful and life-changing, hence not conceiving is comparatively upsetting and life-changing.

SOCIETAL AND MEDICAL FACTORS

Individuals who have never experienced a miscarriage or infertility often find it difficult to comprehend the reason why those affected suffer so greatly. While our society is getting better at addressing the importance and meaning of infertility and baby loss, only those who have gone through it themselves will know what it is like; and even then everyone's experience focuses on different aspects.

When it comes to fertility and having children, it can feel like many have an opinion on the matter and want to share their recommendations. However, advice such as "relax – and it will all be fine", or suggestions to take a holiday, or focus on something different in life and "not be so obsessive about it", can be very hurtful, and make the person suffering feel deeply misunderstood and doubt their own feelings and desires. Some people even believe that treatment for infertility should not be offered by national health services or covered by health insurance as the condition does not have negative physical health consequences. What is often not acknowledged is that the effects of infertility can lead to significant mental health conditions and relationship problems. Furthermore, with declining birth rates and individuals deciding to have children later in life, fertility problems will continue to rise and pose an important medical problem to our society that will need to be addressed.

It can be surprising to find out how many people do suffer from infertility or have experienced a miscarriage. Especially when it comes to miscarriage, many people are not aware of just how common they are. Among women who know they're pregnant, it's estimated about one in eight pregnancies will end in a miscarriage. Some sources state that one in four of all pregnancies end in a miscarriage, as many will happen before a woman even becomes aware that she is pregnant, and hence it might go unnoticed. The main causes of miscarriages have been found to be genetic, hormonal, blood-clotting related, due to infections or due to anatomical abnormalities.

Medicine is only in its beginnings when it comes to fertility problems. There are theories of possible causes of miscarriage and infertility, but investigations are limited and many individuals or couples are left with a vague diagnosis or one of "unexplained infertility" – neither of which feels satisfactory or gives people confidence that their problem can be overcome. Furthermore, interventions and preventions for infertility and miscarriages are generally not as advanced as other medical areas.

The most common intervention for infertility is artificial reproductive technology (ART), such as in vitro fertilization (IVF), regardless of the cause. However, success rates for IVF are fairly poor: in 2018, birth rates per embryo transferred were 25 per cent for individuals aged 35–37, 19 per cent for individuals aged 38–39, and 11 per cent for individuals aged 40–42. In addition, birth rates fall for each consecutive cycle. It is understandable why many who embark on IVF experience great anxiety, as the stakes are high and loss is very possible. Feelings of anxiety or hopelessness make even more sense when considering the great physical, emotional and financial investments a couple makes with each IVF cycle. Each time, there is so much hope pinned on a final successful pregnancy, yet such a high chance that the couple or mother end up leaving this journey empty-handed.

Before we move on to the next part of this chapter, take a moment to check in with yourself about whether you feel you need any further understanding or knowledge about what you are going through while grieving. If you do, go back to chapters 1 and 2.

HOW YOU CAN SUPPORT YOUR OWN GRIEVING PROCESS

I encourage you to follow and use each exercise in chapters 3 to 8, which will help you immensely in your grieving process. In addition, here are some pointers about which areas to pay particular attention to, and some additional tips and advice.

- **Describe your loss** (chapter 4). Having fertility problems will have led to you experiencing a variety of losses. It will help your understanding to be aware of all the areas and aspects of yourself which are affected by your loss, either current or what you had imagined your future or that of your baby would have been like (for example, loss of purpose, loss of becoming a mum/dad, feeling less as a man/woman). It will help you to break things down and grieve each aspect on its own, rather than feeling overwhelmed by wanting to grieve everything at once.
- **Identify the negative belief** you have about yourself in relation to your fertility problems and the **positive belief** you would rather hold about yourself instead (chapter 4). Keep holding the positive belief in mind and review the strength of your negative and positive beliefs throughout your grieving process.

- **Identify and become more accepting of the feelings you are not comfortable with** (chapter 5). Some of your feelings might be unexpected, feel unacceptable (for example envy), overwhelming or deeply upsetting. Helping you to accept them will make it less of a struggle for you to go through your grieving process. Try to ignore others' opinions or judgements about your feelings – your feelings are true and absolutely valid, however strong they are and however long they last.
- **Create a detailed timeline of your loss** (chapter 6), as well as of other pivotal moments in your experience with infertility and/or miscarriage. What is it about your life and experiences that make this loss so painful? Have you experienced an earlier loss? Is having children something no one else in your families have struggled with and you don't understand why this is happening you? Then create your own story.
- **Tell your story** (chapter 7). You might have to/want to tell this many times – there is no limit as long as it helps you to find answers and process your feelings. If you feel uncomfortable sharing it with others, you might want to share it in a supportive online forum for those dealing with fertility problems or miscarriages.
- **Challenge the thoughts and beliefs that keep you stuck** (chapter 7). Any repetitive thought/belief that makes you feel very upset or down is likely one that is unhelpful and will benefit from being challenged. Pay particular attention to unhelpful beliefs about the causes of your problems and how having those problems affects your value as a man/woman.
- **Limit constant searches for certainty and reassurance**. When dealing with fertility problems, it can be easy to become used to constantly "symptom checking" to identify if you are pregnant or if something is going wrong with your pregnancy. Many also fall into habits of searching

the internet for information, causes and solutions to their fertility problems. These behaviours are completely understandable when you are constantly faced with uncertainty and loss. However, it is important for your own wellbeing to limit these behaviours, as engaging in them excessively will ultimately lead you to feeling more anxious and depressed. Whatever you find or notice, you will never feel completely reassured or certain and your fears will increase, which can lead to a vicious cycle, steadily increasing your anxiety and feelings of powerlessness. If you need to, set yourself time limits on how much time you spend on researching your problems/symptoms on the internet, and distract yourself from symptom checking by focusing on other activities.

DEALING WITH FERTILITY PROBLEMS AS A COUPLE

Many couples find that experiencing infertility and/or miscarriages will bring them closer together and find that their partner is the only one who really understands what they are going through and appreciates how difficult it really is. However, in some situations, individuals can experience their fertility problems and losses differently. In addition, every person grieves differently and this can add to a feeling of loneliness and divide in a couple. One of you might want to carry on with their life as "normal" and focus on other things, while the other might feel a need to continue to talk about their feelings and what has happened. One of you might feel deeply affected by having lost a baby, while the other might want to deal with it rationally and see it as "an embryo that was not meant to develop". You might feel depressed and hopeless, while your partner wants to be positive and optimistic for you, or vice versa, which can leave both of you frustrated and feeling misunderstood.

Fertility problems put a huge strain on relationships, and it is only to be expected that even the strongest relationship will struggle at times. If there were problems in your relationship beforehand, these might feel exaggerated due to what you are going through at the moment.

It is crucial for you both to support each other – you are going through this together, whatever your experience. The key is that you learn to respect and validate both of your responses and ways of grieving. Refrain from judging each other, as this is never helpful and will only create a bigger divide between you. Instead, allow each other to feel and respond in the way that you feel is right in this moment in time. When you have opposing needs, try to find a compromise that truly feels doable for both of you. For example, if one of you wants to talk about your feelings and the other one doesn't, allocate a certain amount of time you both feel would be okay to talk about it and then move on to doing something else together. You could also agree that the person wanting to talk more might seek support from others, such as family and friends. The same will work for agreeing on when you are ready to do more enjoyable activities again, or when to have sex again or try for another baby. Find a middle way that will work for both of you, and accept that, in some aspects, you will benefit from seeking support from others and doing activities on your own until your partner feels ready again. You don't have to agree with how your partner responds or feels, nor do you need to convince each other of what is the "right" way to feel or respond. Instead, try to understand each other's feelings and responses and be curious. Your partner will be grateful for your understanding, and it will help you to feel understood by your partner. It will bring you closer together during this exceptionally difficult time and make you feel valued and truly loved.

HOW YOU CAN FEEL POSITIVE ABOUT YOURSELF AND YOUR LIFE AGAIN

Experiencing infertility or miscarriage is devastating, and the pain and loss experienced often lasts years and can, initially, become progressively worse. However, with time, these feelings tend to decrease and become more bearable. Some couples or individuals will eventually conceive and experience a healthy pregnancy that leads to their so-wished-for baby. There is, of course, no guarantee that this will happen, nor will it completely undo all the pain and grief experienced during the time of struggle with infertility or miscarriages. However, many find that the experience helps them to find some kind of resolution and focus on the future with their loved and cherished baby. It's not that the pain or the lost babies are forgotten, but the intense emotions now seem to belong more to the past, while the memory and what one has learnt about oneself continues to live on in a meaningful way.

Some couples or individuals who continue to be unable to conceive or no longer feel they can or want to continue the exhausting process, explore different options to fulfil their desire to become parents and raise a child, such as adoption. Finding another option that feels right can lessen the grief and create new meaning and purpose. However, even if you do not feel that finding a different option to become a parent would be right for you, be assured that most couples and individuals find the strength of their desire to have children decreases steadily with time, until it becomes less and less significant. Reaching this place requires time and patience, and you will only get there once you are ready and have accepted and grieved your many losses.

Coming to terms with your loss, regardless of where you are now or what will happen in the future, can help you to regain a sense of hope and personal strength from having been able to survive this very difficult time. Often, people will feel a sense of relief and a desire to refocus their life on other fulfilling goals once they have found some resolution. What can be particularly helpful is to read about others' experiences of grieving and finding hope and meaning again in their life. It might be particularly difficult for you to imagine how one could ever feel happy and fulfilled again if the desire to have children remains unmet. Reading about real-life experiences can give immense hope and show you that this is indeed possible. You might always feel some sadness and wonder what your life would have been like with a child and as a mum/dad, but the intensity of the grief and sadness will not last and will diminish.

REMEMBERING YOUR BABY

If you have had a miscarriage, or even several miscarriages, you might find that doing something to remember your baby/ies will help you to heal and move through your grieving. There are many things you can do to remember, and it might be useful to listen to what you feel you would like to do and what would make you feel most connected with your baby.

Sometimes hospitals offer a memorial certificate or a scan picture or an entry in a book of remembrance. Even if your miscarriage happened a while ago, it might be useful to contact the hospital to find out what they might offer and what support is available through them.

You might also want to create a memory box with photographs and items that remind you of your pregnancy and your baby. Many find this immensely comforting, and it helps to have a physical representation of what your baby means to you that you can go to and look at whenever you feel you wish to. You might also want to plant a tree or some flowers, either in your own garden or a garden of remembrance. Some parents like to write a poem or a letter to their baby. You might want to get a tattoo, or light a candle in their memory every day to begin with and then later on, on anniversaries and other special days.

Having a funeral or memorial service can also be a useful opportunity to grieve the loss together with others and to commemorate your baby's life. Depending on how old your baby was when you lost her, you might have already had a funeral service soon after the miscarriage happened. However, regardless of whether there has already been a funeral, you may want to arrange a memorial service. You might want to focus your memorial service on what you imagined their character would have been like and the time you had together while you or your partner was pregnant. You can include photos of the pregnancy or when your baby was born and any other memorabilia that has meaning to you. You could hold the service with close friends and family or just with yourself and your partner.

There are many charities that support individuals who have experienced infertility or baby losses, and many find connecting to these charities and joining a support group very useful. Talking and connecting to others who have gone through the same, and understand without judging, can be a huge help with coming to terms with these losses that are often still greatly misunderstood and underestimated by those who have not experienced them.

12

THE END OF A RELATIONSHIP

This chapter is written specifically for someone who has experienced a break-up of a relationship. It will mainly refer to the end of a romantic or marital relationship, but any break-up of a relationship that has caused you great upset and grief will be covered in this chapter. You will benefit from reading this chapter in conjunction with the first eight chapters of this book as they contain further specific insight, advice and exercises to support you and guide you in your grieving process.

WHAT YOU EXPERIENCE AFTER THE END OF A RELATIONSHIP

When a relationship comes to an end, it usually does not happen suddenly; there is often a long period of unhappiness or secrecy that clouds a relationship. Usually, couples will try their best to make it work and spend considerable energy trying to work on their problems. It is only when this fails again and again that one, or both, realize that they have come to a place where there is no longer any hope for their relationship. At other times, one person in the relationship might feel like they have been kept in the dark and are deeply shocked by the other person's seemingly sudden decision to end the relationship.

If you have experienced the break-up of a relationship then the suffering, pain or disconnection one or both of you were experiencing in the relationship had probably become greater than the sense of love, comfort, belonging and any other positive feelings you once experienced. You might have broken up before, but got back together again. Relationships are complex, and no one but you and your partner knows when it is time to say goodbye for good.

Occasionally, a relationship break-up is mutual, but often, one person chooses to end the relationship. Your feelings will be very different if you were the one initiating the break-up rather than the one who will be feeling rejected. If you were the one who decided they wanted to break up, you will likely have come to a place where working on the relationship no longer seemed like an option. You might even feel that delaying would only have further added to everyone's pain. However, if you were the one who was rejected, you might feel that giving up on the relationship was premature, and it might well take you some more time before you will feel able to let go of the relationship completely. You might feel very confused and helpless, and even continue to hold on to some hope that you can get back together again and work out all your problems.

Going through a break-up or divorce is an emotional rollercoaster. Depending on which stage of your grieving process you are in, and which areas of your life have been affected by the break-up, you will feel a range of emotions.

- **Loneliness** – you are no longer able to be close to, or in contact with, the other person; as such, you feel you have no one you can share your most private thoughts and feelings with or be intimate with.
- **Fear** – you are concerned about the future and how to get through the break-up.

- **Anxiety** – you are worried you will never find a partner again, or worry about your age and the implication it will have on the possibility of having a family.
- **Panic** – you experience intense panic and a sense of intense separation anxiety, and feel as if it is impossible for you to cope and exist unless you can be with the person you have lost.
- **Yearning** – you feel a strong desire to get back together again.
- **Anger** – you are cross about what you feel the other person did to cause the break-up, or for them cheating on you or leaving you.
- **Rage** – your ex-partner is conducting themselves badly through a divorce and causing ongoing difficulties for you and insulting you, but you still need to stay in touch to make arrangements about your shared belongings, or custody of your children.
- **Jealousy** – you envy the life you feel they live without you or the partner they are with now.
- **Guilt** – you have left someone and caused them great pain, and you worry how they can cope without you.
- **Sadness** – at some stage in your grieving process, you may feel intense sadness: about all the wonderful times you spent together that will never happen again; about all the time and emotional investment you had in the relationship that now it seems was for nothing; about all the fights and the pain you caused each other; about losing the one person you thought you would share your life with.

There are many more emotions you might experience, of course. Break-ups are complex, and what you experience depends on the circumstances and the relationship you had, as well as your own – and the other person's – way of dealing with difficulties and losses.

In addition to leading to a range of emotions, going through a break-up can be a serious blow to your self-esteem and make you feel worthless and unlovable. Experiencing the rejection, the accusations, the fights and disappointments might initially make you feel as if there must be something very wrong or unlikeable about you for anyone to treat you this way. Rather than feeling that the relationship failed, you might feel that you personally failed. You might conclude that if only you were more valuable, lovable or attractive, this would not have happened.

If you are going through, or have gone through, a divorce or the end of a long-term partnership, the additional task of sorting out shared finances and housing, as well as shared childcare agreements and court proceedings, can be a huge practical and emotional burden. The lengthy process of working out custody and possibly continuing to have regular contact through shared childcare can make the grieving process particularly difficult. Many people find themselves feeling they have never sufficiently grieved their marriage or partnership, and still experience great pain and anger in relation to it.

Before we move on to the next part of this chapter, take a moment to check in with yourself about whether you feel you need any further understanding or knowledge about what you are going through while grieving. If you do, go back to chapters 1 and 2.

HOW YOU CAN SUPPORT YOUR OWN GRIEVING PROCESS

I encourage you to follow and use each exercise in chapters 3 to 8, which will help you immensely in your grieving process. In addition, here are some pointers about which areas to pay particular attention to, and some additional tips and advice.

- **Describe your loss** (chapter 4). The person who you had a relationship with might have taken on many roles in your life and it will help your understanding to be aware of all the areas that are affected by your loss.
- **Identify the negative belief** you have about yourself in relation to your break-up, and the **positive belief** you would rather hold about yourself instead (chapter 4). Keep holding the positive belief in mind and review the strength of your negative and positive beliefs throughout your grieving process.
- **Write down all the things that you are happy to leave in the past.** All the things you will not miss about the person you have lost – perhaps their impatience, the lack of emotional support given, their temper or their refusal to take on responsibilities.
- **Identify, and become more accepting of, the feelings you are not comfortable with** (chapter 5). Some of the feelings people struggle most with after a break-up are loneliness, guilt, panic/fear, shame and anger. Accepting these will make your grieving process less of a struggle.
- **Create a detailed timeline of your loss** (chapter 6). Document the details of how you met each other, the ups and downs of your relationship and the final break-up, and create your own story.
- **Tell your story** (chapter 7). You might have to/want to tell this many times – there is no limit as long as you are finding it helpful. It will help you to get different perspectives, to find answers and to process your feelings.
- **Remember the relationship in a balanced way.** Balance is crucial as you need to allow yourself to grieve the person fully, with all their good and bad sides. It is tempting to see the person we have lost in a break-up in very black-and-white ways (for example, idealizing them if we did not want the relationship to end; or only seeing

their bad side if we experienced a lot of anger and hurt in the relationship. Viewing them in a more balanced and realistic way will help you to feel more at peace with the break-up and see the relationship as a part of your life that you can now leave in the past.

- **Avoid seeing yourself as a victim.** It is important to recognize and acknowledge any pain and wrongdoing you have experienced and not to play this down – however, it's also useful to reflect on what your part was in what happened in the relationship. The purpose of this is not to be self-critical but to help you distance yourself from the victim role that would make you feel resentful, bitter and helpless about what has happened to you, and hence disempowered and stuck.

- **Don't fall into the rumination trap.** It's useful to revisit what has happened to you in a constructive way, to help you come to an understanding of what has happened and come to terms with what you have lost. However, it is not useful to get stuck asking yourself "why" it all happened over and over again, and to keep blaming yourself, as this only leads to depression and a feeling of helplessness. Try to accept that whatever happened, just happened. Rather than "why", ask yourself "how" it happened, and answer the question as truthfully and objectively as you can. It is absolutely normal to remember moments you had together that were particularly pleasant, exciting or made you feel happy, loved and connected. It's part of you grieving the loss of those moments. However, to go over these moments repetitively with the intention of "keeping them alive", rather than grieving the loss, will be less helpful.

- **Challenge the thoughts and beliefs that keep you stuck** (chapter 7). Any repetitive thought/belief that makes you feel very upset or down is probably unhelpful and will benefit from being challenged.

- **Seek professional support and support from friends and charities**. Having to sort out finances, belongings, childcare arrangements or any other legal arrangements can be overwhelming and anxiety-provoking – having people there to provide professional advice and support will help you feel calmer and cope better.

UNFINISHED BUSINESS

Many people who go through a break-up feel that "unfinished business" gets in the way of them fully grieving the loss and moving on from it. This can also lead to excessive rumination and feeling stuck on certain aspects of a break-up. It might be a question they need answers to, wanting an apology or recognition from the other person, or wanting to express something and be heard. If there is any "unfinished business" you feel is keeping you stuck, complete the following exercise to help you find some resolution.

EXERCISE
Unfinished Business

1. Define exactly what it is that you want or are waiting for, that keeps you stuck.
2. Think about what you could do to help resolve it. Jot down several options, if possible.
3. Reflect on which option is most likely going to work and is realistic. You can even write down the advantages and disadvantages of each option.
   Example: If you want your partner to apologize for having cheated on you, but many conversations about this with him/her has never made them

> *apologize, having another conversation with them is unlikely to give you what you need. However, writing them a letter or imagining a detailed scenario during which he/she apologizes might work better and be more realistic.*

These are some ideas for finding resolution to unfinished business that others have found helpful:

- **Writing a letter or email to your ex-partner.** This will help you to get in touch with your emotions and allow you to express what you still want to say to the person, and therefore help to resolve some of your emotions. This can be especially helpful if your ex-partner no longer wants contact with you, or when actual interactions with your ex-partner do not feel constructive and only lead to more hurt or anger. You can then send, keep, delete or bury/destroy the letter/email as you wish.
- **Imagine a conversation with your ex-partner.** Ask them the questions you feel have been left unanswered. Imagine that they are calm and prepared to be completely honest with you as they no longer feel they have to be defensive or hide anything – what would they say? Ask as many questions as you like and express anything you need to; imagine them listening to you fully and taking it all in.
- **Take action.** Is there something you could do or someone you could approach to find your answers?

Once you have done as much as possible, it's important to allow yourself to process whatever you have found and then move on from it. Recognize that you might not find answers to all the questions you had; it is normal to feel there is some unfinished business with every relationship break-up. It's sad and unsettling, and we all wish we could end relationships in peace, having discussed and clarified everything that was left to address and say. However, if you were able to do this with your ex-partner, you probably would have never broken up in the first place! The way to move forward is to do all that you can to find resolution and answers, but then to grieve and *allow* all the feelings you have about any remaining unfinished business. If you follow these steps, you take yourself one step closer to being able to move on from your past relationship.

ESTRANGEMENT

Estrangement is the loss of a previously existing relationship through physical and/or emotional distancing, often as a result of ongoing conflict, traumatic experiences (including violence), fundamentally differing values, severe disappointments, betrayal or mental illness. Estrangement leads to negligible or no communication between the individuals involved for an extensive period of time.

While estrangement can happen in any relationship, people usually struggle with estrangement when it happens within a family system, the most. The separation can often feel unsatisfactory if there was never a clear separation or ending of the relationship, and if either one or both parties never envisaged their loss of contact to be forever. Losing a family member through estrangement is complicated as we know deep down that our father will always be our father and our daughter will always be our daughter regardless of whether we are in contact or not. We cannot simply replace them or become less aware of their existence as we might be able to do when we lose a friend or partner.

Regardless of whether you initiated the estrangement or feel abandoned by someone in your family who no longer wants to be in a relationship with you, you are carrying a heavy burden. You might feel guilty for not being in contact with them and you might feel judged by others for apparently not having made sufficient attempts to reconcile your relationship. In our society, it is often the view that you should forgive and be able to make things work with a family member, no matter what has happened between you. This can be hurtful to hear if you have gone through years of pain and suffering, or if you have made many attempts at connection, which have been ignored consistently.

If you have experienced estrangement and thinking about the person you have lost causes you great discomfort, or you are torn between whether you should get back in contact again or not, you will likely benefit from further grieving the relationship you have lost.

HOW YOU CAN SUPPORT YOUR OWN GRIEVING PROCESS

Most people who have experienced estrangement have never fully grieved their loss. This might be because they never felt that their loss would be final or because their difficult ongoing experiences with the other individual lead to avoidance of engaging with any feelings or memories about them.

Grieving your loss is vital if you want to feel more at peace about yourself and your family. You might feel hesitant to grieve the person as you might feel there is a chance that you will get back in touch at some point in your life. What I would like you to recognize is that the time you have missed with the other person and all the time you have spent suffering in this relationship is already lost, and will always be lost, regardless whether you get back in touch. The missed opportunities, the hurt and the disappointments all need to be grieved. Your relationship will never be the same again and will not continue where it left off. Use all the tips and advice earlier in this chapter and in previous chapters, to help you through your grieving process. Recognize that at this moment in time your loss is definite and clear.

Getting back in touch with the person you have been estranged from is likely to feel very frightening, exciting and hopeful at the same time. I advise you grieve the loss of your relationship before seriously considering attempting any contact with the other person. Your mind will be clouded by strong emotions and anxiety, and it will be difficult for you to make an informed decision unless you have made some peace with your loss.

After you have grieved your past relationships, you might feel ready to leave old feelings behind. Reconnecting with the person you were estranged from can lead to healing, understanding and a sense of returning home. Not getting in touch out of resentment or fear might rob you of the opportunity to make amends and find peace. Of course, there is the danger that making contact will lead to further disappointments and fuel past hurts and memories. Ask yourself what you have to gain and lose from your meeting – honest answers will help you to decide how to move forward.

If you are considering getting back in touch again, it might be useful to consider what you would like the contact to look like – would you like to meet them face to face, talk on the phone or write an email?

What would you like to say to them, or which questions would you like to ask? What are you hoping to gain from your contact? Are your expectations realistic? Would it feel safer for you to take someone with you? How will you cope if the contact does not pan out as you had hoped? Who will support you? Remember that you have a right to set boundaries that feel safe to you – don't let the other person push you to a level of contact that does not feel comfortable; and remember that having made contact once does not mean that you have to stay in contact.

If you are the person who was abandoned, getting back in touch with the other person might be less of an option, or at least it will be less in your control if they have made it clear that they are no longer interested in contact. The best way for you to take back control is to stop waiting for the day they might change their mind. As difficult as this will be, grieving your loss is the kindest and most supportive act you can do for yourself and will be the only way forward. Grieve your loss in every way possible, and then accept that the person is sadly no longer in your life. You have probably done everything you could and now it is up to them whether they want to get back in touch with you – until then, assume that they do not want to.

You might find that grieving your loss is difficult due to something you feel has been left undealt with or some questions you feel you need answers to. If this is the case, follow the advice and exercises on unfinished business, on page 197. The person you are estranged from might not have been a very easy person to be with and it may be useful to follow the advice and exercises in chapter 9, about making peace with difficult relationships.

Once you have grieved the loss of your relationship and detached yourself from the hope that the other person might just change and get back in touch with you again, you will notice a sense of peace and acceptance that your relationship did not turn out as you had wished. From this place, you will be able to start to see clearly who the other person really is, without getting too entangled emotionally. Hoping they will change is likely to lead to more disappointment. In this clear mindset, decide what you do want to do that is healthy going forward. You are only responsible for your own actions, and you have little to no control over those of others. Whatever you do or don't do, whatever you say or don't say, detach yourself from hopeful expectations and feared reactions as much as you can. Whatever the other person does or doesn't do is not your fault or responsibility – you can only act in the way you feel is true to yourself while also caring for, protecting and respecting yourself.

HANDLING A BREAK-UP AND NEW RELATIONSHIPS

If you are still in the midst of your break-up or your divorce proceedings are still ongoing, it's important to have a good strategy in place of how you want to handle your break-up. Take a moment to appreciate what you have been doing well so far, and identify what you would like to change. It is important to recognize that you can only take responsibility for, and control of, what you are doing – how your ex-partner responds and how they conduct themselves is out of your control. Trying to act in a certain way to get a certain response usually only leads to frustration, and can become exhausting. It's completely normal to feel frustrated and that it is unfair that you have to go through this, but it's most helpful to let go of the hope that they are ever going to change.

Consider whether you want to stay in touch with your ex-partner after your break-up. There are obviously situations when you have to stay in touch due to practical reasons, for example, shared childcare; but any contact above and beyond this is up to you and your ex-partner. There is no right or wrong way of how to go about this, and it rather depends on the relationship between the two people, and their individual characters. At the beginning of the break-up, a period of time with no contact can be useful as it will give you the opportunity to fully focus on the initial phases of your grieving rather than getting pulled back into the relationship and continuing the difficulties you were having. However, you might not feel ready to have this break straight away, or you might be forced into a break if your ex-partner does not want any further contact. If you do want to stay in contact in the future or throughout your break-up, be honest with yourself about why you want continuous contact. Do you feel guilty for having rejected them and feel that staying in contact will relieve you of some of that guilt? Do you still want to care for the other, but no longer be in a relationship with them? Is it because they provide you with comfort and support and you don't want to let go of that? Will it just be too painful to think that you might never talk or spend time together again, and staying in touch relieves some of that pain?

Be clear about your reasons and about what messages you send to your ex-partner, and whether this could lead to confusion and further pain. If they read your actions as you still wanting to be with them when you are clear this is no longer the case, continuing any contact might be more harmful for both of you. If you feel that staying in contact with your ex-partner is delaying the inevitable (the pain and grief about the immense loss), you might have to reconsider and plan to take some time apart. You can always become friends at a later stage when you have both done some grieving. If you are both truly interested in a friendship, there is no time pressure on when this will need to happen.

Ultimately, your lives are likely to part unless you start a "different" relationship. If you are able to recognize that whatever relationship you had together has ended and that this will need to be grieved, you will, at some point, be ready to start a new relationship with them. Alternatively, you can come to accept that your partner is no longer part of your life, yet is someone who *was* an important part of your life and who taught you about yourself and what it means to be in a relationship.

Deciding on when to start dating again is an important consideration. Some people tend to start a new relationship as soon as one ends, while others find it difficult to take the first step, and wait years. It's usually advisable to have some time for yourself before starting to date again. You deserve some time to fully focus on yourself, to grieve your loss, and to figure out what you really want for yourself in the future. Identifying what you want your next relationship to be like will help you to be aware of falling into old patterns, such as behaving in a way that you know contributed to the pain and upset you experienced in your old relationship, or getting involved with someone who is unable to offer you what you are really looking for. Making time for reflection and discovery will help you avoid future pain and repeating the issues of your last relationship. However, avoiding dating for a long time after your break-up might be driven by fear, and will prevent you from possibly finding a fulfilling relationship and sharing joy, love and excitement with another person.

Grieving the break-up of a relationship can take a long time. Often, people wish they weren't still upset about the end of their relationship after several months, or believe that they should have been able to move on. However, having shared so much, and having been so close and important to each other, it is understandable that it will take time to withdraw all the energy and emotional and practical investments you made in the relationship and make peace with what has been lost. It is only when you have fully grieved your last relationship that you can fully engage in a new relationship. Many people will start a new relationship before they have grieved their last one – and that is absolutely okay – but it's important to continue your grieving process and be aware of triggers and feelings that belong to your previous relationship. A lack of awareness can often lead to you blaming your new partner or asking them to repair something that has nothing to do with them.

HOW YOU CAN FEEL POSITIVE ABOUT YOURSELF AND YOUR LIFE AGAIN

Once you have gone through the most intense phase of your grieving process, your emotions about the break-up and what you have lost will have lessened. What will be very useful for you – if you have not already done so – is to start working on remembering your relationship in as balanced a way as possible. Those who move on from a break-up and feel happiest in the long-term are those who can take this step and feel grateful for what they had in the relationship, but also see all the negatives about the relationship in a realistic way. Most people find that once they have grieved the loss of their partner sufficiently, they are able to think about the other person without feeling overly sad, anxious or angry, and without having a great need to either re-connect with them or block them out of their mind completely. It is a feeling of having made peace, of having left the relationship in the past and moved on from it.

Working through this book has hopefully helped you to get closer to this state of mind. Here are some other things you can do to help you feel better about yourself and your life again.

RECONNECTING WITH FRIENDS

A break-up is a huge loss and sometimes people describe the feeling of loss as close to what one would feel after a person dies. In some way, what you are experiencing is the loss of the presence of the other person. They do live on, but no longer with you. From the early stages of your grieving process, it is important to surround yourself with good friends... Friends who will be happy to listen to your story and your heartache, or your ongoing frustrations with your ex-partner. Friends who will take your side and be there for you when you feel lonely. Friends who will take you out and help you to reconnect to what it is like to have fun. Experiencing how others value you greatly after having felt deeply rejected by another person can be very healing and self-assuring. Depending on your situation, you might feel guilty for reaching out to friends again if you had less time for them during your relationship. Please do not let your guilt get in the way of reaching out – most people understand that being in a relationship means you spend less time with friends and more with your partner, and they will be happy to support you during such a difficult time.

IMPROVING YOUR SELF-ESTEEM

Your self-esteem will likely have suffered as a result of your break-up, and you might be blaming yourself for a variety of things. If you think that your self-esteem has not been affected, but you are still not feeling yourself again, reflect on how you really feel and be completely honest with yourself. Sometimes it is hard for us to admit vulnerability, or we hide behind blaming everyone else for what went wrong in order to protect ourselves from a sense of failure and worthlessness.

Regardless of how you feel, improving your self-esteem after a break-up (or at any time, for that matter!) is a great idea. Use some of the extra time you have at hand to concentrate on yourself. There are many great books on how to improve your self-esteem, and many tips and ideas you can find online, such as through TED talks. Here are some ideas to help you improve your self-esteem.

- **Every day, make a list of three things you feel you have done well that day.** This could be completing a difficult or challenging task; looking after your health through exercise or healthy eating; being supportive or nice to a friend; reflecting on difficult feelings or writing in your journal. Spend a moment to really sense what it feels like to have accomplished each item on your list. Do you feel proud, fulfilled, joyful, calm?
- **Learn to recognize and deal with your inner self-critic.** Notice when you start to criticize yourself. Usually, when you speak to yourself in a harsher tone than you would to anyone else, your inner self-critic is talking. It's often fruitless to try and negotiate with or convince the inner self-critic that they are wrong, as this will only spur them on. Instead, try to listen to what they have to say, recognizing that their view is always exaggerated and fear-driven, and focus on intention rather than what is actually being said. For example, if the inner self-critic is telling you that you are stupid, take it as a reminder of how important it is for you to do well and not let others get the better of you, but that "stupid" is clearly an exaggeration and you do not need to listen to insults. What will also help is to reassure your inner self-critic that you can ensure that you do well and not let others get the better of you in ways that do not involve insulting yourself, for example with positive encouragement, rather than criticism. Your inner self-critic might welcome a break from having to work so hard all the time!
- **Identify the negative belief** you generally hold about yourself as a person, and define which **positive belief** you would like to hold instead (chapter 4). These might be the

same beliefs you hold about yourself regarding your loss, but they might also be different. Rate how strongly you hold each belief from 0 to 10. Go back to chapter 4 for a list of negative and positive beliefs you might hold about yourself. Then challenge your negative core belief and find evidence that this is not true. Likewise, find evidence and examples for why your positive core belief is true. Use evidence and examples from your past and your present. Rate your beliefs again and identify any shift. You can do this exercise several times, and even use it at the end of each day to find evidence for each belief from your experiences during the day.

- **Spend time with friends and family.** Having people around us who care for us and love us is a brilliant self-esteem booster. If you feel comfortable, share with them that you are working on improving your self-esteem and ask them what they most value about you. You might be surprised by how much they have to say.
- Remember and say this quote to yourself whenever you feel your self-esteem is low: **"Self-esteem is the ability to see yourself as a flawed individual and still hold yourself in high regard."** (Terry Real). It's not about being perfect or doing everything well, but it is how you relate to and support yourself while trying your best.

LEARNING FROM YOUR PAST RELATIONSHIP AND STARTING A NEW RELATIONSHIP

Reflecting on your past relationship and seeing it as a learning experience can help you feel more positive about what has happened to you, even though the outcome was not as you had hoped it would have been. We all have to learn to have healthy relationships, and our learning lasts our whole life as we encounter different challenges and life stages. When looking back at your relationship, ask yourself the following questions. Take your time to find your answers; sometimes you might not be sure, and it will be useful to come back to it again at a later stage.

1. What is most important for me in a relationship?
2. What is it I missed most in my last relationship?
3. What are the things I keep encountering in relationships that I struggle with?
4. What was my part in how the relationship unfolded?
5. What are the relationship patterns I usually find myself in? *Example: Are you a rescuer and often date people who have difficulties you end up helping with? Or do you always end up feeling emotionally neglected and misunderstood? Have you been cheated on or do you often fear your partners are unfaithful? These are only some examples of many possible patterns.*
6. What is the type of person I am usually attracted to? How has this affected my relationships?
7. Going through each of the answers from question 1 to 6, what would I like to be different in my next relationship? What will I need to do to make this happen?

I want you to allow yourself to really engage with these two last questions and write down everything that comes to mind. It might be difficult to think about what needs to be different, or you might find it a challenge to find all the responses you are looking for. However you feel, allow yourself the time you need for your answers to develop and your learning to become clear.

Once you have some clarity about your past relationship/s, take this opportunity to make a conscious choice to work on yourself and your relationship patterns. You cannot change another person, but you can be more mindful about the types of partners you get involved with. You can also be more aware of how you behave in relationships, and which of those behaviours make it more difficult for you to have the loving relationships you long for and deserve. Make this time you have by yourself truly special and you will see the benefits in the future.

A word of caution: relationship patterns can often be complex, and if you find it hard to see what is getting you into the same old patterns again and again, or you struggle to identify how to make changes, seek support from a therapist specializing in relationships, who can help you work through things.

Only you will know when is the right time to start a new relationship. What most people find useful, but is not always easy of course, is to not focus too much on the need to find a suitable partner in order to feel complete or happy again. Plan your life and live it as fully as you can without constantly feeling you are waiting for the right person to come along. Your life is hugely valuable and complete the way it is now, and another person or relationship will not make your life more valuable than it already is. Many people hope that a relationship will fix certain feelings or problems, but usually they don't. Constantly focusing on what you are missing in life is only going to make you feel lonelier and more depressed. I know, it's easier said than done! But be mindful of your thoughts, and try to shift your focus and perception at least some of the time.

When you do meet new people again, try to enjoy the process and don't get too hung up on the end goal. Putting too much pressure on yourself to find the right person and to be in a relationship again will often cause so much anxiety that people find it hard to actually start dating, and are a lot more tense during the initial stages of dating, which then makes it harder to get to know someone else.

Meet different people in whichever way you find comfortable. You might find it useful to think about dating as "relationship practice" – wouldn't it be great if you could practise your relationship skills so you then feel much more confident once you meet a person who is right for you?

13

JOB LOSS, REDUNDANCY AND RETIREMENT

This chapter is written specifically for someone who has experienced the loss of a job or employment. You will benefit from reading this chapter in conjunction with the first eight chapters of this book, as they contain further specific insight, advice and exercises to support you and guide you in your grieving process.

WHAT YOU EXPERIENCE WHEN YOU LOSE YOUR JOB OR EMPLOYMENT

Losing your job or employment can be a great blow to your self-esteem. When we are content at work, we experience a sense of identity, of self-worth, of belonging and of fulfilment. Work provides us with financial stability, recognition and purpose. When you lose your job, your losses are far-reaching and significant. Don't underestimate how losing all the aspects connected to your working life, as well as the job itself, can cause you to feel deeply sad and lost. Losing your job will destabilize you emotionally and practically and might leave you with fears about how you will look after yourself and your family. You may have many fears about the future and how to cope with everything going forward. You might feel intense anger about the causes or people behind you losing your job, or about how unfair it is that this is happening to you and not others. Ultimately, losing your job will often feel like a failure; it can make you feel ashamed of yourself and lead to you severely doubting your abilities, your worth and your identity.

There are many different ways to lose your job – redundancy, chosen or forced retirement, ill-health, relocation, transfer, business closure – and none is worse or easier than the other, rather it depends on what it means to you personally and your circumstances.

Job losses happen much more frequently these days than they did 50 years ago. To understand why this is the case, and to help you reflect on the meaning you attribute to losing your job, it is useful to look at how our relationships with work, employers and employees have changed significantly in our society in the last century.

People used to live and work in the same place for most of their life, and would often be closely connected or even work with their families. It was not unheard of for a person to work for the same company their whole life; even changing positions and promotions were less frequent and less expected. Today, we want flexibility, opportunities and to be valued and promoted by our employer. If a job does not fulfil our sense of purpose or identity, we often decide to leave companies and colleagues behind. Emotionally, we are much more invested in our work and because we invest more, we expect more back. The difficulty is, we have come to expect our employers to provide us with an opportunity to grow and develop and give us freedom, yet also expect them to provide us with stability. We want a sense of belonging and support, but also to be able to revoke it at any time. Companies and work structures have changed immensely, and we would probably say that these changes have been necessary and many are for the better – creating more opportunities, more equality and more fulfilment at work. However, the loss of stability and security in our working lives is a side effect that we perhaps did not intend. These changes mean we have to get used to the experience of losing our job, and become more confident in dealing with this particular kind of loss. This is by no means an easy task when so much of our identity, wellbeing and security seems highly dependent on our work.

Losing your job through retirement is different, in that the loss of one's job and profession is not limited to a certain amount of time that will eventually be replaced by starting a new job. Retirement – for many of us, at least – is final and can lead to a loss of purpose, belonging and self-worth. It can create a sense of emptiness and be a prominent reminder of entering the later stages of your life. As such, it brings you in contact with a whole range of losses you experience as you grow older, as well as with your own mortality. You might experience retirement as losing part of your identity that was closely connected to your profession, and a sense that your standing in society has somehow diminished now that you no longer work. The routine and direction that was once provided by your job will be missing, and some struggle to find new routines and give their life direction again.

Before we move on to the next part of this chapter, take a moment to check in with yourself about whether you feel you need any further understanding or knowledge about what you are going through while grieving. If you do, go back to chapters 1 and 2.

HOW YOU CAN SUPPORT YOUR OWN GRIEVING PROCESS

I encourage you to follow and use each exercise in chapters 3 to 8, which will help you immensely in your grieving process. In addition, here are some pointers about which areas to pay particular attention to, and some additional tips and advice.

- **Ensuring your basic needs are met** is key before you can start any work on grieving the loss of your job and move on to find a new job or profession. If finances are a problem, sit down and have an honest review of your finances and essential monthly outgoings. Make a plan of how you can make ends meet for the next two to four months and explore all options. Are there any government support schemes or benefits you can access? Can you defer mortgage payments? Are there any other costs that can be cut? Don't hesitate to ask your partner/spouse or family members to help out financially while you are going through this very difficult time. Having a robust plan in place will help you reduce your anxiety significantly and allow you to fully focus on coming to terms with the loss of your job and finding a new one.
- **Describe your loss** (chapter 4). Your job might have had many different meanings to you and it's helpful to be fully aware of all the aspects you have lost before you can grieve each of them. It might have given you purpose, a feeling of success, respect, authority, self-esteem, credibility, financial security and a sense of belonging. It might have held a promise for your future professional development, or you might have invested a lot into it, which now all seems to have been lost.
- **Identify the negative belief** you have about yourself in relation to the loss of your job, and the **positive belief** you would rather hold about yourself instead (chapter 4). Keep holding the positive belief in mind, and review the strength of both your negative and positive beliefs throughout your grieving process.
- **Identify and become more accepting of the feelings you are not comfortable with** (chapter 5). Some of the feelings people struggle most with after losing their job are anxiety, anger, low mood, hopelessness and shame.

Accepting them will make it less of a struggle for you to go through your grieving process.

- **Create a detailed timeline of your loss** (chapter 6). Include details about any parts of your educational or professional history that are relevant, and create your own story.

- **Tell your story** (chapter 7). You might have to/want to tell this many times – there is no limit as long as you are finding it helpful. It will help you to find answers and to process your feelings.

- **Remembering the job you have lost, including the company, any managers and colleagues, in a balanced way will support your grieving process and help you to move on.** There is no need to see any difficult managers or dysfunctional companies in a positive light or to paint a job you truly loved in a negative way, but it will be useful to see everything in perspective and try to understand the bigger picture. For example, why your manager behaves in a certain way or how a certain industry or sector operates. You don't have to agree with it, but gaining perspective will help you to distance yourself from it.

- **Challenge the thoughts and beliefs that keep you stuck** (chapter 7). Give particular attention to the unhelpful thoughts you have about why you have been made redundant, such as "I am worthless/a failure", "I am dispensable" or "I should have worked harder". In addition, identify and challenge any negative automatic thoughts you have about your future, which will be making it so much harder for you to move forward.

- If your working life has ended due to retirement, attending retirement planning workshops, either offered by your employer or through private organizations, can be very helpful and encouraging. These training sessions usually address your feelings as well as practical aspects about your retirement, and will give you an opportunity to meet others going through the same process.

- If you are unsure about how to progress in your career or working life, it might be useful for you to book some sessions with a career coach, who can help you identify obstacles, suitable career paths and advise you on which steps to take next. Having someone who is an expert to go through this difficult journey with and give you a helping hand can make things a lot easier. Likewise, if you want to start your own business, there are many clubs and coaches that can support you through the initial processes and make sure you take into account everything that is needed.

IMPROVING YOUR SELF-ESTEEM

Your self-esteem will likely have suffered as a result of having lost your job, and you might feel that ultimately you have failed as a person. Our self-worth is tightly caught up in our work. The ability to support ourselves and our family greatly depends on having a source of income, and we spend a huge part of our life at work or working. So, it's not surprising our self-esteem is negatively affected when this significant and vital part of our life is suddenly taken away. Improving your self-esteem will help you to cope better emotionally while unemployed or during the early stages of your retirement, and will also help you with finding a new job or new goals in life. To find help with improving your self-esteem, turn to chapter 12, page 207, where you will find useful tips and exercises.

HOW TO MANAGE YOUR TIME WHILE UNEMPLOYED AND LOOKING FOR A NEW JOB

It's important to make a good plan for how you want your day-to-day life to be while you are coming to terms with the loss of your job and searching for a new one. Having lost your job will mean that your routine will have changed drastically, and this can be very disorienting and easily lead to difficulties with managing and allocating your time, as well as to procrastination. Hence, planning and deciding on a new routine is crucial. Make your routine as realistic as possible, and review it along the way as your needs will change. Consider yourself to be still working – you are not on holiday or a planned sabbatical (I know you probably wish you were...), and you still have lots of important work to do. Your work now is to grieve the loss of your old job and look after your mental wellbeing as well as you can, and to find a new job or start a new career. There is lots to do!

Get a weekly planner and plan each day and week ahead, including all the tasks you want to accomplish. Be sure to include fun and social activities, just as you always used to. Try not to spend too much time on the latter as this can become a way of avoiding your grieving or dealing with your current problems, but likewise don't restrict any pleasurable activities for any reason, for example because you feel you no longer deserve them or would feel ashamed to meet with others. Getting out of the house and being around people regularly is vital for your physical and mental wellbeing. It might feel difficult at times as it might remind you of how others are still going to work and following their usual daily work routine, but it will feel easier with time. Remember that the work you are doing at the moment is just as valuable and important as the work someone does who has a paid job.

Stay in contact with your friends and meet up with them regularly. Again, this can feel hard when it feels their time is limited due to work and other commitments, while you suddenly have a lot of time on your hands. Having a range of friends and family members you can be in touch with is often the best solution. Try to avoid checking your phone too often, and focus on your "work" during the day without letting yourself get too distracted.

To help you set up a routine for your time being unemployed and looking for a new job, go back to chapter 3. This chapter will help you to include all the important aspects in your routine, including grief time, looking after your physical health, pleasurable activities and rest/sleep. Add to these the time you will spend on any activities related to finding a new source of income. Remember to set up SMART goals to learn any new skills and to plan activities to help you find a job (see pages 146–147). This might include reflecting on your career path and your profession in general, and where you would like to go to next. It will include analysing the current job market, talking to peers in the industry you are interested in, researching and completing any relevant training, looking for and applying for jobs or working on your own business plan.

When you choose to start activities related to finding a new source of income is up to you, and also depends on your personal situation. It's advisable not to rush things – allow yourself to grieve your loss for some time before throwing yourself into a new job. That said, it's often not realistic for people to wait too long; financial pressures may allow little time for grieving their loss. If this is the case for you, make sure that you allow some time each day for your grieving process. If you don't, your emotions are likely to build up and lead you to feel increasingly anxious, depressed or on edge. Feeling this way will not be sustainable in the long-term, or help you find a job or start a different career.

HOW TO MANAGE AND PLAN FOR YOUR RETIREMENT

Retirement will lead you to experience practical, financial and emotional changes. Many people think about the financial impact of retirement, and planning for this largely means looking at your expected outgoings and income through pensions or other sources when you are retired, and making sure that you will be able to cover all your costs. Practically, you might want to move to a different area or downsize/upsize.

What many people do not realize is that it is also important to plan what to do with all the additional time one will have available. Initially, it might be a relief to no longer have to go to work each morning and come home tired every day, and to have all this free time. However, many people who retire can experience a sudden feeling of emptiness and loss of purpose when they realize they have no important tasks to accomplish or hobbies to fill their time. Many people will live for 30 years or more after they retire, so it's important to see retirement as a period of your life for reflection, developing yourself and finding new areas you want to dedicate your time to.

To help you start structuring and filling your time with meaningful activities, make a plan of three things you would like to concentrate on going forward. Think about the interests and hobbies you would like to explore, or the sports and projects you never had time for during your working life. Perhaps you want to contribute or volunteer in your community, or write a book or join a drama group? Perhaps you want to travel, or run your first half marathon or go back to studying? It's never too late to start anything!

Make sure you keep in touch with friends and family, and you can make new friends by attending classes, social groups or getting involved in your community. It's easy to feel lonely as you get older and no longer have daily contact with people through work. Make sure you start building a solid social support system now.

Emotionally, make sure you spend time on your grieving process, using the suggested exercises in chapters 3 to 8. Once you feel ready, it will be useful to think about the losses you have experienced and to look for other areas or activities that will help you to regain some of the things you have lost. For example, if you have experienced a loss of identity, see if there are any activities that will require you to use your professional skills and knowledge. If you miss a sense of purpose, volunteering or helping out in your community could fill that need. You won't be able to replace all the losses you have experienced, of course, and it will never feel quite the same as it did when you were working, and this should not be your goal. Whatever you have lost is, unfortunately, gone. Instead, you might find that you will discover new positives and opportunities about your life that you will find fulfilling.

HOW YOU CAN FEEL POSITIVE ABOUT YOURSELF AND YOUR LIFE AGAIN

Following on from grieving the loss of your job, adapting to and coping with the changes in your life will help you to feel more positive and at peace with these changes. Ultimately, this will lead you to feel more positive about yourself and your life again.

The loss of your job, and either starting the search for a new employment or starting your retirement, is a huge change; it will demand a considerable amount of time and energy to process, and to adapt to your new situation. Once you can appreciate what the change in situation will require from you, and are able to see it for what it is, rather than trying to minimize or exaggerate the task at hand, you will start to feel more confident and calmer about being able to get through this. Of course, the whole process will be frightening and uncomfortable at times, but you will be able to manage difficult times by taking things step by step and following the advice in this chapter.

Remember, if you feel that you would benefit from more help with how to cope with all the change resulting from the loss of your employment, it might be useful for you to revisit chapter 8.

Most people will feel positive and happy again once they have a vision for how their working or retirement life can feel fulfilling and stable again, and they have the skills and confidence to put their vision into practice. For others, happiness will also be linked to finding some resolution or new routine that will be sustainable and fulfilling. For you, this might mean finding new goals and purpose during your retirement, finding new employment, embarking on a path that will led to a new career, or starting your own business.

Losing your job is terribly unsettling and destabilizing. Outwardly, it looks like a very negative experience to go through. However, with time, you might start to view your situation more positively. You might start to appreciate that this change – even though it may not have been of your own choice – posed an opportunity for growth, self-actualization and reflection on who you really are and what is important in your life. Sure, being thrown into the deep end will feel very uncomfortable at first, but sometimes we need to be pushed to find the courage to start new things and explore new avenues. I am not saying you should not feel sadness, anger and anxiety about having lost your job, but once you have engaged with all those feelings and moved on in your grieving process, there will be a time to open yourself up to the positives that have come through this very important change in your life.

14

SIGNIFICANT ILLNESS, INJURIES AND LOSS OF HEALTH

This chapter is written specifically for someone who has had a significant injury or has suffered from a significant illness. You will benefit from reading this chapter in conjunction with the first eight chapters of this book, as they contain further specific insight, advice and exercises to support you and guide you in your grieving process.

WHAT YOU EXPERIENCE AFTER HAVING HAD A SIGNIFICANT INJURY OR ILLNESS

Losing part of your health through an injury or an illness is a terrible experience, and the effects will often be significant and lasting. Recognizing what has happened, and what this will mean for your own future and that of others, might feel very bleak to start with. However painful it feels, it is important to recognize what a difficult situation you are really going through. Engaging with those feelings might make your illness or injury more "real"; it will help you to acknowledge and fully accept how you really feel about what has happened to you, so you will be able to move forward and find ways of grieving your loss, as well as finding new hope for living a happy life.

SECONDARY LOSSES

If you have experienced a loss of health, your life has probably been turned upside down. When your health is affected in a significant and possibly even chronic way, or if you have been given a terminal diagnosis, you are faced with a huge challenge to come to terms with your numerous and overwhelming losses.

- You might experience disability and hence **loss of your physical capabilities, financial losses and a loss of purpose, status and belonging.**
- A loss of health can also lead to a **loss of employment and a loss of relationships.**
- As your physical and mental wellbeing is so closely related to your identity, any significant loss in your wellbeing often also leads to a huge **loss of self-esteem and loss of self.** Considering the vast effects an illness can have on a person, it is easy to understand why some feel like they are no longer themselves, but have been reduced to their medical condition.
- Significant mental illnesses and addictions can lead to an even greater **loss of personality, loss of self-esteem and loss of loved ones** as well as a **loss of happiness and sense of mental and physical safety.**

EMOTIONAL REACTIONS

Emotionally, your life will be greatly upset, especially if your illness was unexpected or has a significant effect on your ability to cope physically or mentally on your own. Many will experience strong and overwhelming feelings that will make them feel quite helpless or even depressed.

- It might be difficult to imagine that anything might ever feel better again when you are coping with the immediate aftermath of a serious injury or a significant illness.

- You might experience anger or intense frustration with your situation, your medical team or those around you as you struggle to come to terms with what has happened to you.
- You might be in denial about the consequences of your illness, and avoid speaking about it with others or attempt to continue your life as before.
- You might feel intense sadness about losing your health, and the subsequent secondary losses.
- It might be intensely painful to realize that those things will be lost forever or that a significant part of your life will be spent fighting or dealing with your illness.
- You might feel numb or depressed about your life and yourself, and feel a crushing absence of positive feelings or hope for your future.
- You might feel very anxious about many things. How will you cope with all the emotions, the pain, the financial impact? How will your illness or injury progress? How will your family and friends react to your losses, and will they still care for you and love you as much as they did previously?
- A loss to your health can feel quite shameful, as it can affect your ability to function, physically and mentally.
- You might feel a strong resistance to even considering grieving or coming to terms with your loss as you fear that it will all be too overwhelming and hopeless, or because engaging with it will mean accepting what you wish not to be true.

Grieving your innumerable losses will likely feel impossible to start with. In addition, the task of grieving can be particularly difficult when you are not well mentally or physically.

Be patient with yourself, and remember that many others have been able to grieve their loss of health and even find meaning in their experience, learning to live a fulfilled and happy life, even if they felt completely hopeless to start with. It's not going to be easy, and it will take time – depending on your illness or injury it could take many years – but you will get there.

Before we move on to the next part of this chapter, take a moment to check in with yourself about whether you feel you need any further understanding or knowledge about what you are going through while grieving. If you do, go back to chapters 1 and 2.

HOW YOU CAN SUPPORT YOUR OWN GRIEVING PROCESS

I encourage you to follow and use each exercise in chapters 3 to 8, which will help you immensely in your grieving process. In addition, here are some pointers about which areas to pay particular attention to, and some additional tips and advice.

- **Develop new routines and a comprehensive self-care plan** (chapter 3). Your life is likely to have changed considerably, and your routines and needs will be very different than before. Finding new routines and putting them into practice will help you to feel calmer and more in control. Looking after yourself and attending to all your basic needs, as outlined in chapter 3, is now more important than ever. Looking after yourself – as difficult as it might be at times – is non-negotiable, and needs to be your top priority to get through this difficult time and help your body and mind to heal.
- **Describe your loss** (chapter 4). Significant illnesses and injuries cause innumerable losses, and it will help your understanding to be aware of all the areas that are affected by your loss. It will help you break things down

and grieve each aspect on its own, rather than feeling overwhelmed by wanting to grieve everything at once, without being clear what you are actually grieving.

- **Describe the person that you thought you were, or were going to be, before you had your injury or developed your illness.** What did you imagine your life would be like? What were your hopes and dreams? Part of your grieving will involve grieving your future and the person you imagined you would have become without your illness. Allow yourself to feel all the emotions you have about losing that part of yourself, all the difficult changes and a possible deterioration.
- **Identify the negative belief** you hold about yourself in relation to your injury and illness, and the **positive belief** you would rather hold about yourself instead (chapter 4). Keep holding the positive belief in mind and review the strength of both your negative and positive beliefs throughout your grieving process.
- **Identify and become more accepting of the feelings you are uncomfortable with** (chapter 5). Until you have fully experienced all of your anger, sadness and anxiety, you will find it hard to move on and find lasting hope and enjoyment in your life again. It's normal to be in denial about your situation and feelings for a while, but suppressing your feelings in the long-term is likely to disempower you. Supressing your feelings will keep you stuck as you will likely avoid any situations that would make your illness more real and bring on emotions. Alternatively, you end up being depressed or stuck in guilt and anger about what happened to you, as these are the only emotions you are comfortable with. It's incredibly difficult to be with all the emotions that will arise in you, but the more you allow them to be there, the easier it will get and the less powerful they will become.

- **Improve your abilities to cope with your anxiety** (chapter 7). Anyone who is faced with a significant illness or has experienced a severe injury will feel very anxious at least some of the time. It's completely normal to feel this way, and sometimes your anxiety will energize you to find the right treatment and solutions to help you recover and make important changes in your life. However, when your anxiety becomes debilitating, it's important to deal with your stress; follow all the tips and advice in chapter 7. Most importantly, learn to let go of your worries and learn to accept uncertainty.

- **Plan and engage in activities that bring you meaning and joy.** It will help you to keep focused on what you as an individual are really about, and not let your injury or illness take over your life. What brings you joy is deeply personal, but can include anything from taking classes, joining a club, spending time in nature, enjoying the arts or being creative yourself. Your condition might have changed the activities you are still able to pursue, or might even have changed your interests – take this as an opportunity to explore new activities or interests, and seek inspiration from others.

- **Create a detailed timeline of your loss,** especially of when you received your diagnosis or realized how serious the illness is and how it will affect your life. Then create your own story (chapter 6).

- **Tell your story** (chapter 7). Telling your story will help you to find answers and to process your feelings. Injuries and illnesses are deeply personal, and some people find it difficult to talk about them, and their feelings, with others. You might also worry that others do not want to hear the painful or sad story about your many losses, and would prefer to focus on keeping positive about the future. Choose someone you can trust and ask them if they would be happy to listen to your story. You can even write it down and send it to them if you feel more comfortable doing so, but make sure you have some face-to-face time with them after they have read it. Most of the time, people will feel truly honoured that you chose to share your story with them.

- **Challenge the thoughts and beliefs that keep you stuck** (chapter 7). Any repetitive thought/belief that makes you feel very upset or down is likely to be unhelpful and will benefit from being challenged. Be particularly mindful about thoughts and beliefs about the illness/injury being your fault or that you deserve it. Forgive yourself if you think you have made mistakes in dealing with your illness, or if you think you could have prevented your injury. Severe illnesses and injuries do happen, however hard we try to avoid them.

- **Be patient with the pace of treatment and your recovery.** It can take time and many medical investigations for you and your medical team to find the right course of treatment and support, or to settle on a prognosis. It's easy to become anxious when you are faced with uncertainty or you wish you could channel more focus and energy into your treatment but you are still waiting for your doctors to identify what this will look like. Illnesses with a terminal diagnosis are particularly difficult as deterioration is a given, but it is often difficult to predict when this will happen. Try to focus on what you have control over and what you can do to help enhance the quality of your life, such as grieving your losses, developing and sticking to your self-care plan, doing the things you love and enjoy, and staying connected to family and friends.

REACHING OUT FOR SUPPORT

When you have to cope with a significant illness or injury, reaching out for support is absolutely essential. You might be the type who has never felt comfortable asking for help, or are too proud to ask for support now. You might also fear that you will be a burden, or that others will not be willing or able to help.

Whatever worries are on your mind, acknowledge those worries and how hard this is for you, and then move on and reach out for help regardless. This is not the time to retreat into a shell. Your wellbeing depends on having a good support system in place. Having someone to talk to and express how you really feel whenever you need to can have a huge positive impact on your mental health. Likewise, having someone to take you to medical appointments or help with chores or tasks can help you to feel less alone with what you are going through.

Your relationships may well change – you will get closer to some people and more distant from others. Try not to get too hung up on those who struggle to form a new relationship with you – it's nothing to do with you, but is mostly about their own fears and feeling helpless. Most people will feel honoured by your trust and will do their best to help you.

If possible, try to see people face-to-face as much as you can. The support you feel and the positive effect it has on your wellbeing when you have a person close to you is much greater than receiving messages or talking on the phone.

If you feel that you do not have support in place, remember that there are many different ways to grow your social support system. Family and friends are often the first ones you might be thinking about when considering support. However, having the right medical team, including physiotherapists, nurses and even psychologists, is just as important. You might also want to receive support from charities who offer support for people who have your illness or have suffered your injury. There are many specific organizations that offer peer-support programmes, and match you with a person who is living with the same type of medical condition; this can help you to get invaluable insight and advice regarding your condition and how others cope with it. Some people also find it useful to see a counsellor or psychotherapist to help them come to terms with what has happened. Having someone who is professionally trained to help you with your emotions and make sense of what has happened without judging you, or you having to worry about how they are affected by what you are telling them, can be immensely useful. They will help you to not drown in your despair and depression, to not be overwhelmed by your anxiety, and to find a way forward.

Choose the support that is right for you at this moment in time. Don't worry too much about what others think you need – only you know your situation and what you need. If you would like to get more insight and advice about reaching out for support, revisit chapter 3.

COPING WITH CHANGE

Being diagnosed with significant and lasting health problems often means that your life will change entirely in ways that you had never anticipated. Experiencing change that you feel you have no control over, that happened unexpectedly and that will require you to adjust significantly, is the hardest challenge to deal with.

However, you will be able to cope with these changes. While it might be difficult for you to truly believe this when you are just starting to get to grips with this tragic situation, remember that there are many things you can do to better deal with your situation. It will likely take time for you to find your own solutions and ways of handling things, and you might have to try a few options until you find the right one for you.

Remember that your loss of health – as with every other loss you experience in life – will require time for you to process, and is going to result in changes that you will need to adapt to as part of the grieving process. Adapting to your new reality and all the changes usually happens after or alongside expressing and engaging with the emotions surrounding what has happened to you. Coping with your new situation will require you to accept what has happened and be prepared to be open to new ways of living and to adapting your hopes for the future. This often includes a period of learning new skills and testing out new ways of living. It will also include reviewing your hopes and dreams, letting go of those that no longer fit your life and replacing them with new hopes and dreams.

As we covered in chapter 8, the whole process of change involves ways of coping with your emotions, dealing with difficulties and taking appropriate action to adapt to your new reality. Return to chapter 8 to remind yourself of the knowledge and skills, as well as the exercises, that will help you to better cope with your change. It will also be very useful for you to remind yourself how to increase your confidence by setting up a realistic action plan to acquire new skills, which will help you to embrace your new reality. It will be particularly useful to increase your knowledge and skills on your particular illness or injury, using trustworthy sources of information. This will help you feel empowered and more in control when talking with professionals about your condition, and will enable you to be actively involved in deciding what care is best for you.

Have a go at exploring opportunities your new situation has to offer. Don't worry if you are finding this difficult, or you can't think of many at this moment in time. Think of any dreams or ideas you have – old ones or new ones – that you might want to pursue. Perhaps there is an activity or interest that you have always wanted to do and realize it is important to you to make it a priority now.

HOW YOU CAN FEEL POSITIVE AGAIN

Feeling positive about yourself and your life can sometimes take time, and your journey is likely to have many ups and downs. It's a great challenge to live with a serious health condition, especially if your prognosis is unfavourable.

Please believe that – whatever your condition or prognosis – it is possible to get through this and to have a happy and fulfilling life, as long as you allow yourself to grieve all your losses and you are willing to open up to all the changes you will need to adapt to. It may not be easy or straightforward, and it is likely to take time, but you will get there.

To feel positive again, looking after your physical and mental health is an absolute priority and will provide you with a good basis from which you will be able to find meaning and joy again.

It will also be vital for you to hold on to yourself as an individual whose values, characteristics, uniqueness and core essence have not changed, regardless of how your illness or injury has affected you. You are so much more than just your condition, and it is important to focus on this in your daily interactions and relationships. Of course, this can be challenging when you are constantly reminded of your ill health due to medical treatments and how it is affecting your day-to-day functioning. However, focusing on your core personality will help you to distance yourself from your illness or injury at times. When interacting with others, make sure you let them know when you want to focus on you as a person, and your relationship. It can be difficult for others to know how much they should ask about or talk to you about your health, and they often appreciate guidance.

One of the biggest challenges will be to adapt to the huge changes in your life and the losses you will experience in relation to your past, but also your future. There may be a part of you that will resist any change, will not want to accept the losses, and will feel angry and sad about why this has happened to you, and fearful of the future. All these emotions are a natural reaction to what you are going through. Feeling and expressing those feelings will help you to move on, even if it seems counterintuitive at first. Only when you have grieved your losses will you feel open to discover and engage with your new opportunities and embrace your new reality. You can be in touch with all your negative feelings about your ill health and at the same time feel positive and open toward adapting to your new life. You might even discover that many of your dreams and hopes might still be possible – even if slightly different to what you had imagined.

Some people who have faced great adversity and ill health decide to use and channel all the energy and time they have on what is really important to them and find great meaning and purpose in how they live the rest of their life. Depending on your condition and your prognosis, feeling positive about yourself and your life in your situation might always have a bittersweet feeling. However, you might become deeply aware of, and connected to, the value and meaning of life, which will open you up to experiences and emotions that might have been hidden to you previously.

Thinking about the future when your life has been turned upside down takes a lot of courage. I want you to trust yourself and believe that you have the courage it takes to feel positive again and to cope and adapt to all the challenges you are facing. Be patient with yourself, trust your resilience, and be open to whatever changes your condition has presented you with. You can do this.

PART 3

LOOKING FORWARD

15

PLANNING FOR THE FUTURE

Before we look at how you want to plan for your future and continue your grieving process, I want to congratulate you for having done so incredibly well already!

By reading this book, educating yourself, doing the exercises and learning new skills, you have given yourself the best chance of getting better and feeling more like yourself again. Immersing yourself in the grieving process gives your brain the best opportunity to deal with and move on from your loss. Even if you feel that improvement has been slow, or you wish you had come further by now, remember that everything you have learnt and read will continue to have a positive influence on how you feel and how you interact with yourself and others. Sometimes we are unaware of how something affects and helps us, and it is only over time that we realize the full effect.

By now, you will probably have realized and become comfortable with the idea that getting better does not mean that things will be as they were before, rather that you will be returning to a new, different normal. A new normal that you might still need to adapt to but that perhaps you will grow to appreciate to some degree.

Many people find that after they have grieved their loss, felt their emotions about their loss intensely, and gone over what happened many times, there comes a time when the intensity and frequency of their emotions naturally lessens. It's almost as if there comes a time when all your emotions have run their course and you will want to stop hurting. It will feel natural to recognize that your loss is in the past, and that you can take whatever good you have learnt from your experience – or from who or what you have lost – forward, while letting go of anything you no longer need.

You might already be there, or perhaps you feel that have more grieving to do to get to this place. Whatever you feel – empathize with your struggles, while also acknowledging your achievements.

So again – well done! Your dedication has been truly amazing.

Now, let's look at the exercises, skills and insights you have found most helpful and how far you have come to reach your goals and in changing the negative belief about yourself toward a positive belief. I will also help you to identify what you will benefit from working on going forward, and help put a plan in place to put this into practice.

WHAT HAVE YOU LEARNT AND WHAT WOULD YOU LIKE TO TAKE WITH YOU GOING FORWARD?

I would like you to spend some time reflecting on what has been most useful for you about working through this book. Is there any insight or knowledge you have found especially enlightening? Were there any exercises or strategies you found particularly helpful? Take your time and refer to your notes and journal entries; we tend to remember the more recent insights and exercises (naturally!), and you might have forgotten about an earlier chapter or exercise that really helped you to move on in your grieving process. It's useful to identify three to five insights/exercises/skills and make a note of them.

While you are reflecting on all your amazing work, you might also want to ask yourself if you want to revisit some of the exercises that you might have skipped if you felt they were irrelevant at the time or seemed too difficult – you might find that how you feel about them has shifted.

IAN'S STORY

Ian was diagnosed with recurrent depressive disorder a year ago after having struggled for years, and his relationship of three years also ended shortly afterwards. What he found most useful and wished to take forward after having worked through this book was learning about the functions and importance of emotions, including depression. He also found it insightful to recognize that being diagnosed with an illness is a huge loss that requires a period of grieving and adapting. He found the exercise about devising a timeline of his losses and writing his own story very difficult, but also very helpful – finding themes and connections gave him a better understanding of what he had been through, and felt very cathartic and empowering to him.

Ian was surprised to identify his negative core belief as "I am a burden", in both of his losses and many other areas in his life. This discovery provided him with hope that he could work toward feeling "I am valuable" (his wished-for positive belief), although he feels there is more work to do to reduce the intensity of his negative belief.

Ian noticed that he had merely skimmed through the chapter on coping with change – he did not do any of the exercises, as he did not feel ready to fully accept and adapt to his losses and "new reality". Being completely honest with himself, he knows now that he will need to address his difficulties with change, and that adapting to his new life will be crucial for him to move forward. Reflecting on this, Ian now feels ready to read the chapter again and try some of the exercises.

REVIEWING YOUR GOALS AND BELIEFS ABOUT YOURSELF

I would like you to take this moment to rate your goals and beliefs about yourself again for the very last time as far as following this book goes!

REVIEWING YOUR GOALS AND PROGRESS

Date:

Rate on a scale of 1–10 to what extent you feel you have already reached these goals, where 1 means not at all and 10 means completely:

My first goal is: _____

Rating: /10

My second goal is: _____

Rating: /10

My third goal is: _____

Rating: /10

Negative belief: _____

Right now, how disturbing does it feel to think of the worst part/ moment of your loss and the negative belief about yourself? Rate on a scale of 0–10, where 0 means no disturbance at all and 10 means the most disturbance you can imagine.

Rating: /10

Positive belief: _____

How true does the positive statement feel to you right now when you think about your loss? Rate on a scale of 1–10, where 1 means not true at all and 10 means completely true.

Rating: /10

EXERCISE
Reviewing Your Progress

To review your progress, take some time to answer the following questions in your journal:

1. Which goals have you been able to make the most progress with?
2. What effect has improving or even achieving these goals had on you and your emotions?
3. What have you learnt about yourself that you wish to hold on to?
4. In addition to the goals you identified in chapter 4, have you achieved something else you did not expect? If so, make sure to make a note of it!

When looking at the ratings above and any additional goals you might have achieved, are you happy about how far you have come? If you are, you have every reason to be! If you are not, do you tend to have high expectations of yourself and be self-critical, focusing on what you have done badly rather than what you have done well? If this is the case, I invite you to be aware of these tendencies, and flip it around by focusing on what you have done well and how good this feels. Focusing on what you have gained will motivate to increase your gains and energize you, whereas criticizing and minimizing achievements will only zap your energy and lower your mood and self-esteem.

Generally, people find that when working on specific goals and changing core beliefs about themselves, they make very good progress in one area, medium progress in most others, and little or no progress in a few. Coming to terms with your major loss and adjusting to your new reality is a slow and gradual process. It takes time to grieve and to change your core beliefs about yourself, and hence to reach your goals. Therefore, it is expected that you might still wish to improve on some areas or on how you feel about yourself. Remember that working through this book is about putting in place important foundations, and that you will continue to improve and achieve your goals every day as you have internalized a lot of useful knowledge and skills.

We will be looking at "troubleshooting" your progress in more detail, but it's worthwhile to reflect now on what might have contributed negatively to progress toward your goals. Have new obstacles arisen that you could not have foreseen? Were your goals realistic? Do your goals need to be adjusted to make them more realistic – more relevant to you – now? Sometimes, with time and processing our losses, our needs and wants change, and it is only natural that our goals can also change as a result of this.

Likewise, perhaps you have made good progress on reducing the strength of your negative belief about yourself and increasing the corresponding positive belief, but you might have discovered that there is a different negative belief that is now troubling you. If this is the case, you might want to focus on reducing the new negative belief going forward and finding a corresponding positive belief that you want to work toward.

Ian made the most progress on the following goals:

GOAL	INITIAL RATING	CURRENT RATING
"It is not that I don't hurt, but the hurt now is limited, manageable, and understood."	1/10	5/10

GOAL	INITIAL RATING	CURRENT RATING
Negative belief: "I am a burden."	8/10	3/10
Positive belief: "I am valuable." (Both in relation to the break-up of relationship. Ian has been finding it harder to make a shift in his core beliefs regarding his depression.)	2/10	8/10 Ian has recognized that his previous partner could be quite critical and unsupportive, and that his friends valued him whether he was depressed or not.
New goal/achievement: Feeling less depressed	Ian noticed an unexpected improvement in his depression – the number of days he feels depressed and the intensity of his depression has lessened. Ian attributes this to having learnt new techniques and ways to accept and cope with his emotions, as well as to spend time exploring and really understanding his problems, and having had positive experiences of support and understanding from his friends.	

NEXT STEPS

We will now look at what would you like to continue to work on, and devise the best plan of action. If you are struggling with planning for the future or do not feel very positive about what you have achieved so far, you might want to read *Troubleshooting* on page 249 first.

EXERCISE
What I Would Like to Continue to Work On?

1. Taking into account what you have reflected on and identified in this chapter already, write down any goals – old or new – you would like to achieve or

further improve on. This might include a goal about increasing a positive belief about yourself (and reducing the corresponding negative one).

2. To further identify what is important to you and what you might want to add to your list of areas to focus on going forward, ask yourself:

   o What did you find most challenging about grieving or working through this book, and why do you think this was? Would you like to overcome this challenge?

   o Are there any particular emotions, memories or situations you find hard to shift and which frustrate you? Which emotions would you most like to see a shift in?

   o Which parts of your loss have you accepted and which parts remain stuck? Your answers will lead you to the areas where your grief has not yet been resolved, and the feelings that still need to be expressed.

3. Once you have answered the above questions and reflected on them together with the initial goals/ areas you identified, I want you to decide on three main goals you would like to achieve or continue to improve. Make sure these are "SMART goals" (see page 147).

Example: One of Ian's SMART goals is to "decrease the negative belief about myself that 'I am a burden' when I think of having recurrent depression from 7/10 (current rating) to 3/10." He would like to achieve this within the next six months.

EXERCISE
Devising a Plan of Action for your Future Goals

Now let's look at what will be your best plan of action.

First of all, reflect on and brainstorm how you might best achieve your goals. If you need some help coming up with solutions, here are some questions to help you identify what might be most useful (only answer those relevant to you):

- Could any of the exercises and skills you identified as most helpful earlier in the chapter help you to achieve or improve on any of your goals?

- Are there other exercises or skills in this book that could help you work toward any of your goals?

- Might there be a chapter in this book you would benefit from reading and working through again?

- How confident are you in accepting and expressing your emotions? Are there any particular emotions you struggle with and would like to become more confident with?

- What do you think might help with increasing your acceptance? Perhaps exercises from this book (in particular in chapters 5 and 7)? Or engaging or facing situations that get you in touch with those emotions?

- Have you found it useful to journal and/or take notes while working through this book, or have you found this difficult and not written down very much? Might you benefit from writing more things down going forward?

- Might you simply need more time to achieve your goals, and therefore just continue what has been working for you so far?

- Might you be in need of support to achieve your goals? If so, what kind of support do you need and who could offer this to you? Your partner, a friend or perhaps a therapist?
- Are you in need of a "break" from actively working on achieving your goals? Depending on how much time and effort you have put into working through this book, it can sometimes be beneficial to take a step away and allow yourself a break before returning with a fresh outlook and a new perspective.

Considering your answers to the questions, write down an action plan of how to achieve or improve on each of your chosen three (SMART) goals. There is no need to make this plan complicated or long. Look at each goal and choose one to three key strategies that you believe will help you toward achieving this goal. The strategies will be made up of any actions you have identified.

Example: Ian made the following action plan to achieve his goal... "Decrease the negative belief about myself that 'I am a burden' when I think of having recurrent depression.":

- Give myself more time to journal about and engage with my feelings regarding my loss of health/ depression using the exercise in chapter 5.
- Read and work through chapter 8, "Coping with Change", again. I know I need to adapt my life and how I look after myself if I want to keep well and reduce my depressive episodes.
- Seek support from my closest friends to help me challenge and reassess my belief that "I am a

> burden", especially in relation to my depression
> – possibly by talking through the memories and
> parts of my depression I find most distressing
> and shameful.

TROUBLESHOOTING

If you feel that you have not made as much progress as you had hoped to after working through this book, or if you are lacking confidence about whether you have been using this book as well as you could and about how to plan for the future, it will be useful to look at what might be causing you to feel this way.

It is easy to blame yourself for not spending enough time or making enough effort to achieve your goals and work through your grieving process. Alternatively, you may think that perhaps this book is not very good and that the suggested techniques don't work. There can, of course, be some truth in both statements, but from my experience these are things we easily tell ourselves and they are not very constructive – things are usually more complex.

To find out what else might be going on and help you find constructive solutions to your lack of confidence and achievement, let's explore what else might have got in the way.

Let's look at some areas and problems that can add to the feeling you are not making enough progress, and the actions that will help you to overcome this feeling:

PROBLEMS WITH DEFINING AND ASSESSING GOALS

Being completely honest with yourself, answer the following questions:

- Were your goals realistic?
- Were your goals clearly defined and achievable in the time you gave yourself?
- Are you focusing on what you haven't achieved rather than what you have?
- Were your expectations realistic, taking into account the severity of the impact of your loss?
- Have you given credit to any unexpected improvements in your life?

We all hope to get better as quickly as possible, and sometimes cannot bear to imagine that this might take quite some time. As a result, we can be overoptimistic in our expectations and so set ourselves up to fail. Some people also find it difficult to clearly define their goals. Measuring any improvement can be very subjective, and lead you to judge yourself unfairly, rather than looking at the facts.

Action: Revisit your goals and achievements, and make adjustments as needed. Review your progress, trying to focus on your gains rather than what you haven't achieved yet. When planning for the future, make sure you set realistic SMART goals and come up with an action plan that makes you feel confident and inspired to make progress in those areas.

DIFFICULTIES COPING WITH SETBACKS

It's a common reaction to feel like giving up when we face setbacks. We like to hold on to the fantasy that our improvements should be linear and that, if we try hard enough, we will be rewarded with positive results. The truth is that improvement is hardly ever linear, and it's completely normal to have times when you improve a lot and times when you see no improvement at all, or even feel worse for some time. There are so many factors involved in reaching your goal, and many are out of your control. What you do have control over is your commitment to working through your grief and not getting caught up in your natural ups and downs – and then, I guarantee, you will make progress.

Action: Make a commitment to stay focused on achieving your goals, regardless of how many setbacks there will be. Ask yourself what might help you to feel more confident about coping with ups and downs, and reflect on how you have dealt with setbacks in the past. Do you have memories of giving up and/or memories of sticking to your goals? What approach helped you to persist and not give up or feel deflated? What helped you to get through and overcome your setbacks? Then put these insights and coping strategies into practice.

NEGATIVE SELF-TALK

Many people struggle with negative self-talk, especially when they are feeling low or going through difficulties. Talking negatively to yourself can take many forms, and might not always be obvious. For example, if you put yourself down and show little patience toward yourself or if you tend to focus on your failures rather than your achievements, you are engaging in negative self-talk. It is, of course, normal to sometimes talk to yourself in a critical way in moments of frustration or despair. However, when this becomes a habit, and you sincerely believe that these statements are true, then it is a problem. You might feel that giving yourself a telling off or focusing on what you haven't achieved will "jolt" you into action or keep you motivated and focused. But, honestly, how successful has this approach ever been for you? Does it keep you motivated and energized, or does it make you feel low and like giving up, and like a failure? If negative self-talk does work for you, carry on; but if it doesn't, you need to change to a way of talking to yourself that will help you feel motivated and energized, and therefore help you to achieve your goals.

Action: Approach your progress with curiosity, compassion and understanding. Focus on what has been going well and try to learn from these experiences. Acknowledge your achievements and allow yourself to feel good about them.

Likewise, acknowledge the struggles you have been having; but rather than putting yourself down and blaming yourself, try to be curious and really understand why things might have been so difficult and what might be getting in the way of moving forward. Be compassionate about your struggles and your regrets, and show empathy toward yourself. Acknowledge how hard you have tried, and how painful it is to not to have made the progress you wish you had.

Once you have allowed all your feelings about your difficulties and regrets, and you have come to an understanding and acceptance about why this might have been the case, decide on your constructive action to move forward. Then, continue to work on achieving your goal. Approaching your difficulties in a positive and constructive way might even help you to find different, more effective solutions to your problems.

DRAWING UP YOUR PLAN

To summarize all the key learning from this chapter so far and your plan going forward, please complete the activity box that follows. Please feel free to add more than three items to each category. You can use this summary as a simple reminder of your plan for the future and to remind you how best to continue working through your grief.

MY PLAN GOING FORWARD

The most important things I have learnt and want to take forward:

1. _____

2. _____

3. _____

I feel the greatest sense of achievement about having improved on the following goals:

1. _____

2. _____

3. _____

I want to continue working toward achieving the following (SMART) goals:

1. _____

2. _____

3. _____

My action plans to achieve these goals are:

1.

  1.1 _____

  1.2 _____

  1.3 _____

2.

  2.1 _____

  2.2 _____

  2.3 _____

3.

  3.1 _____

  3.2 _____

  3.3 _____

16

FINDING MEANING

Planning for the future involves thinking about how you want to feel about yourself and your loss once your grieving has brought you to the point where you are at peace with how your life has changed. Finding meaning in your loss can help you to reach this point, and/or finding meaning can naturally happen once you have fully grieved your loss.

Finding meaning takes time and is a very personal thing. You might not find it until months or years have passed since you experienced your loss. The meaning you attribute to your loss will be personal to you, and does not need to make sense or be valid to anyone else. Meaning cannot be forced, and will develop naturally. When you find your own meaning, it will never make up for all the loss and pain you have experienced, nor will it make the loss worthwhile. A loss will never feel like a gift or a blessing, but neither is it there to test you.

Meaning is simply what you make of your loss that brings you peace and allows you to appreciate how precious life is and to be in touch with the deeper meaning of your life.

Unfortunately, there is no exercise or technique for finding meaning in your loss. It will naturally develop when you are ready to engage with it and your pain has run its course, allowing you to move on and see your loss in a different light. However, you might have an idea or inkling about what meaning your loss might have for you in the future, or perhaps you have found some meaning already. Finding meaning can take many shapes and forms. Below are some examples of the meaning others have found in the losses they have experienced.

- Feeling gratitude for the time you had with the person you lost and everything you have learnt from them.
- Finding rituals that help you to commemorate and honour the person or thing you have lost.
- Developing a greater appreciation for life and for those parts of yourself unaffected by your loss.
- Developing greater understanding and compassion toward others who have gone through something similar to you; helping and supporting others to overcome their pain and find meaning again.
- Being more in touch with the brevity and value of life, and how this has positively changed your actions, focus and perception of yourself and others.
- Deepening of your nourishing personal relationships and helping you to find the clarity and strength to end those that were harming you.
- Opening up of new possibilities – or exploring parts of yourself – that would otherwise not have been discovered by you.

You can use your journaling time or times when you feel naturally peaceful and in touch with life – such as in a beautiful place in nature – to allow yourself to open up to any meaning you can find in your loss.

FINAL WORDS

The sadness about your loss and the yearning for what once has been and no longer is might always be there with you. But by fully grieving it, and with time, it will no longer feel so intense; it will become more of a memory, a momentary feeling, rather than the focus of your life.

Finding meaning and feeling positive about yourself and your life again are the final stages of your grieving process. Once you are there, you will feel alive and aware of all the beauty around you again.

Wherever you are right now with your loss and grief, and however far you still have to go, remember that getting to that positive place is where your grieving journey will take you.

ACKNOWLEDGEMENTS

My deepest gratitude goes to all my clients who have invited me into their worlds and have shared their stories and most private thoughts and emotions with me. You have made it possible for me to expand my own internal world and understanding, and this book would not have been possible without you.

Thanks to my teachers and supervisors who have taught me how to fully appreciate and understand what it means to be human and make sense of all the complex emotions and experiences we have. I am so grateful for everything you have taught me, and for your ongoing inspiration and support.

Thanks also to Lauren Callaghan, clinical psychologist and co-founder of Trigger, for providing me with this invaluable opportunity. Thank you for your belief and trust in me – now and in the past. Your achievements, energy and expertise are truly amazing.

Thank you to my editor Beth Bishop for her positivity, professionalism, encouragement and trust in my abilities. Thank you also to everyone at Welbeck Publishing Group who has guided me through this process, helped me to organize my thoughts and made this book a possibility. It's been such a pleasure to work with you.

To my beautiful friends Ewa, Zeynep and Katja. I cannot describe in words how valuable your understanding, support and belief in me throughout my life has been.

To my partner Tom – you mean the world to me. To my adorable and amazing son Frederick and our beautiful baby boy who will be with us very soon – I cannot wait to meet you. You remind me every day of what is most important in my life and how grateful I am for everything I have.

ENDNOTES

1   Parkes, C M, *Bereavement: studies of grief in adult life*, Routledge, 2001
2   Keedwell, P, *How Sadness Survived: the evolutionary basis of depression*, CRC Press, 2008
3   Tedeshi, R G & Calhoun, L G, "Posttraumatic Growth: Conceptual Foundations and Empirical Evidence", Lawrence Erlbaum Associates, 2004
    Linley, J, "Positive change following trauma and adversity: a review", *Journal of Traumatic Stress*, 17, 11–21, 2004
4   Kübler-Ross, E, *On Death and Dying*, Routledge, 1969
5   Rando, T A, *Treatment of Complicated Mourning*, Research Press Publishers, 1993
6   Stroebe, M & Schut, H, "The dual process model of coping with bereavement: rationale and description", *Death Studies*, [Online] 23 (3), 197–224, 1999
7   Ibid.
8   Worden, J W, *Grief Counseling and Grief*, Springer Publishing Company, 1992
9   NatCen Social Research, *Predicting wellbeing*, retrieved from natcen.ac.uk/media/205352/predictors-of-wellbeing.pdf, accessed 11 April 2021
    Teo, A R, "Social Relationships and Depression: Ten-Year Follow-Up from a Nationally Representative Study", PloS one, [Online] 8 (4), 2013
    Santini, Z I, Koyanagi, A, Tyrovolas, S, & Haro, J M, "The association of relationship quality and social networks with depression, anxiety, and suicidal ideation among older married adults: Findings from a cross-sectional analysis of the Irish Longitudinal Study on Ageing (TILDA)", *Journal of Affective Disorders*, 179, 134–141, 2015
10 Rando, T, *How to Go On Living When Someone You Love Dies*, connect.legacy.com/inspire/grief-recovery-learning-to
11 Ford, L, "The psychological health benefits of accepting negative emotions and thoughts: Laboratory, diary, and longitudinal evidence", *Journal of Personality and Social Psychology*, [Online] 115 (6), 1075–1092, 2018
12 Shapiro, F. (2006). New notes on adaptive information processing: Case formulation principles, scripts, and worksheets.
    Hamden, CT: EMDR Humanitarian Assistance Programs
13 Anon (2013), *Diagnostic and statistical manual of mental disorders : DSM-5 / [American Psychiatric Association ; DSM-5 Task Force]*, 5th ed. Washington, DC: American Psychiatric Association.
14 Ibid.
15 ICD-11 for Mortality and Morbidity Statistics (Version: 09/2020), icd.who.int/browse11/l-m/en#/http%3a%2f%2fid.who.int%2ficd%2fentity%2f1183832314
16 Ibid endnote 13.

USEFUL RESOURCES

RECOMMENDED READING

Beck, JS, *Cognitive Behavior Therapy*, Guilford Press, 2011

Devine, M, *It's OK That You're Not OK*, Sounds True, 2017

Fennell, M, *Overcoming Low Self-Esteem*, Robinson, 2016

Gilbert, P, *Overcoming Depression*, Robinson, 2009

Kessler, D, *Finding Meaning*, Rider, 2019

Kolk, B, *The Body Keeps the Score*, Penguin, 2015

Law, R, *Defeating Depression*, Robinson, 2013

Leahy, R L, *The Worry Cure*, Piatkus Books, 2006

Levine, P A & Frederick, A, *Waking the Tiger*, North Atlantic Books, 1997

Morris, S, *Overcoming Grief*, Robinson, 2018

Padesky, C A & Greenberger, D, *Mind Over Mood, Second Edition: Change How You Feel by Changing the Way You Think*, Guilford Publications, 2015

Stone, H, *Embracing Your Inner Critic*, HarperOne, 2011

Ward, B, *Healing Grief*, Vermilion, 1993

GRIEF, LOSS AND BEREAVEMENT

8 Pillars of Strength: juliasamuel.co.uk/pillars-of-strength. A self-help framework to find the attitudes, the ways of being and the good habits that will help build resilience to manage the highs and lows of the grieving process. Written by Julia Samuel, psychotherapist and author of grief literature.

Cruse Bereavement Care: www.cruse.org.uk. Charity offering information and bereavement counselling.

The Good Grief Trust: www.thegoodgrieftrust.org. Information, advice and encouraging stories from others.

Help Guide: www.helpguide.org/home-pages/grief. Coping strategies to deal with a variety of losses, including illness, job losses, losing a pet and the break-up of a relationship.

Modern Loss: modernloss.com. Candid conversations about grief.

Mindfulness and Grief: mindfulnessandgrief.com. Meditation, yoga and journaling resources.

What's Your Grief: whatsyourgrief.com. Online community for grieving people.

BABY LOSS

The Miscarriage Association: www.miscarriageassociation.org.uk. Provides information and support to help those who have or are experiencing a miscarriage or molar/ectopic pregnancy.

Tommy's: www.tommys.org. Provides pregnancy information and research, especially in relation to baby loss. The website has lots of useful information and support for those who have experienced baby loss.

Still Standing Mag: stillstandingmag.com. For all who are grieving child loss or infertility.

RELATIONSHIPS

Relate: www.relate.org.uk. The UK's largest provider of relationship support, offering information and advice regarding how to deal with the break-up of a relationship, as well as well as being single or starting a new relationship.

Citizen Advice: www.citizensadvice.org.uk/family/ending-a-relationship. Practical advice on how to end a relationship and sort out things like money, children and your home.

JOB LOSS, REDUNDANCY AND RETIREMENT

Age UK: www.ageuk.org.uk/information-advice/work-learning/retirement. Financial, practical and emotional advice on how to prepare for your retirement.

SIGNIFICANT ILLNESS, INJURIES AND LOSS OF HEALTH

Marie Curie: www.mariecurie.org.uk. Charity providing a wealth of information and support to people living with a terminal illness.

Disability Horizons: disabilityhorizons.com. Providing practical information and emotional support to those living with a disability.

MENTAL HEALTH HELP

UK

- Anxiety UK: www.anxietyuk.org.uk
- Get Self Help: www.getselfhelp.co.uk
- Heads Together: www.headstogether.org.uk
- Hub of Hope: hubofhope.co.uk
- Mental Health Foundation UK: www.mentalhealth.org.uk
- Mind UK: www.mind.org.uk
- Rethink Mental Illness: www.rethink.org
- Samaritans: www.samaritans.org, helpline: 116 123
- Scottish Association for Mental Health (SAMH) (Scotland): www.samh.org.uk
- Shout: www.giveusashout.org, text 85258
- Young Minds: www.youngminds.org.uk

Europe

- Mental Health Europe: www.mhe-sme.org
- Mental Health Ireland: www.mentalhealthireland.ie

USA

- Anxiety & Depression Association of America: adaa.org
- HelpGuide: www.helpguide.org
- Mentalhealth.gov: www.mentalhealth.gov
- Mental Health America: www.mhanational.org
- National Alliance on Mental Illness (NAMI): www.nami.org
- National Institute of Mental Health: www.nimh.nih.gov
- Very Well Mind: www.verywellmind.com

Canada

- Anxiety Canada: www.anxietycanada.com
- Canadian Mental Health Association: cmha.ca
- Crisis Service Canada: www.ementalhealth.ca

Australia and New Zealand

- Anxiety New Zealand Trust: www.anxiety.org.nz
- Beyond Blue: www.beyondblue.org.au
- Centre for Clinical Interventions:
  www.cci.health.wa.gov.au/Resources/Overview
- Head to Health: headtohealth.gov.au
- Health Direct: www.healthdirect.gov.au
- Mental Health Australia: mhaustralia.org
- Mental Health Foundation of New Zealand:
  www.mentalhealth.org.nz
- SANE Australia: www.sane.org

TriggerHub.org is one of the most elite and scientifically proven forms of mental health intervention

Trigger Publishing is the leading independent mental health and wellbeing publisher in the UK and US. Clinical and scientific research conducted by assistant professor Dr Kristin Kosyluk and her highly acclaimed team in the Department of Mental Health Law & Policy at the University of South Florida (USF), as well as complementary research by her peers across the US, has independently verified the power of lived experience as a core component in achieving mental health prosperity. Specifically, the lived experiences contained within our bibliotherapeutic books are intrinsic elements in reducing stigma, making those with poor mental health feel less alone, providing the privacy they need to heal, ensuring they know the essential steps to kick-start their own journeys to recovery, and providing hope and inspiration when they need it most.

Delivered through TriggerHub, our unique online portal and accompanying smartphone app, we make our library of bibliotherapeutic titles and other vital resources accessible to individuals and organizations anywhere, at any time and with complete privacy, a crucial element of recovery. As such, TriggerHub is the primary recommendation across the UK and US for the delivery of lived experiences.

At Trigger Publishing and TriggerHub, we proudly lead the way in making the unseen become seen. We are dedicated to humanizing mental health, breaking stigma and challenging outdated societal values to create real action and impact. Find out more about our world-leading work with lived experience and bibliotherapy via triggerhub.org, or by joining us on:

🐦 @triggerhub_

ⓕ @triggerhub.org

📷 @triggerhub_

9 781837 963485